DIANA SOUHAMI

COCONUT CHAOS

Diana Souhami (signature)

DIANA SOUHAMI

COCONUT CHAOS

Weidenfeld & Nicolson

LONDON

First published in Great Britain in 2007
by Weidenfeld & Nicolson

Lyrics on p.78 used by courtesy of Bocu Music Ltd,
1 Wyndham Yard, London W1H 2QF.
Photocopies of this lyric are not permitted.
Composers: Bjorn Ulvaeus and Benny Andersson.

ISBN 978 0 297 84787 8
Printed in Great Britain by Butler & Tanner Ltd, Frome and London
Design and illustration by Peter Campbell

Weidenfeld & Nicolson,
The Orion Publishing Group Ltd
Orion House,
5 Upper Saint Martin's Lane,
London WC2H 9EA

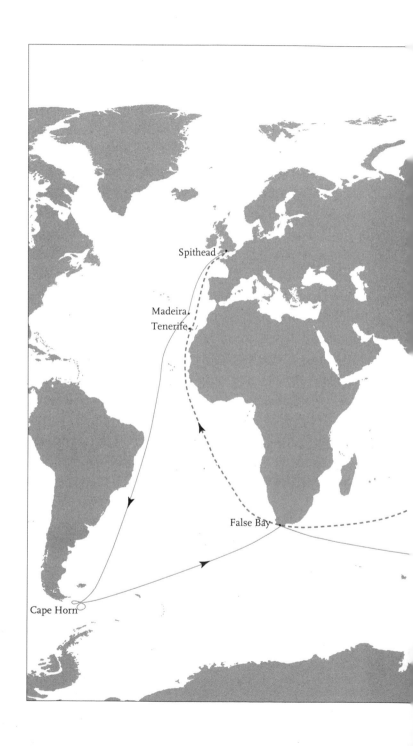

Spithead

Madeira
Tenerife

False Bay

Cape Horn

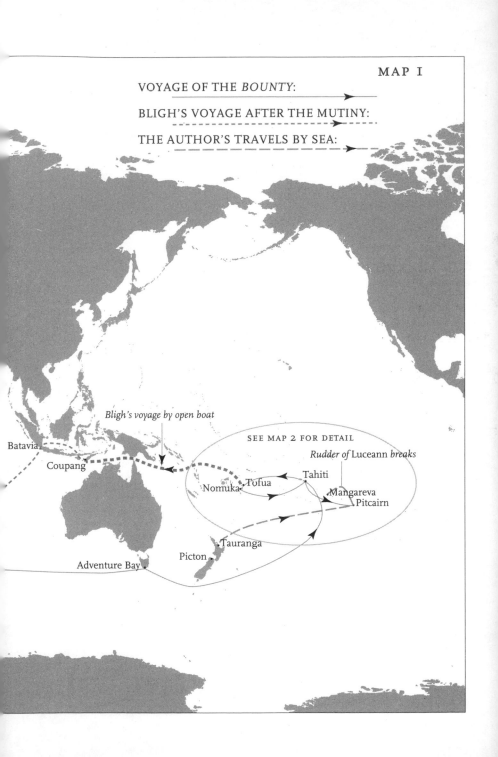

MAP I

VOYAGE OF THE *BOUNTY*:

BLIGH'S VOYAGE AFTER THE MUTINY:

THE AUTHOR'S TRAVELS BY SEA:

SEE MAP 2 FOR DETAIL

Bligh's voyage by open boat

Rudder of Luceann *breaks*

Batavia

Coupang

Nomuka

Tofua

Tahiti

Mangareva

Pitcairn

Tauranga

Picton

Adventure Bay

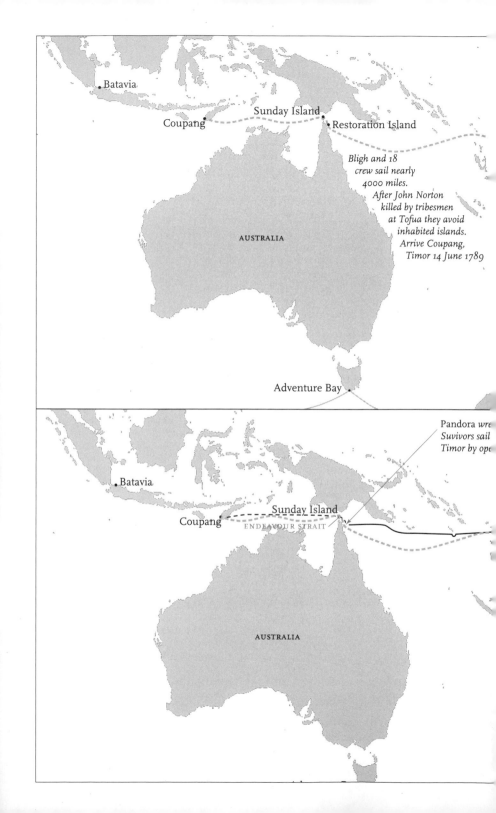

Batavia

Coupang

Sunday Island

Restoration Island

*Bligh and 18
crew sail nearly
4000 miles.
After John Norton
killed by tribesmen
at Tofua they avoid
inhabited islands.
Arrive Coupang,
Timor 14 June 1789*

AUSTRALIA

Adventure Bay

Pandora *wre
Suvivors sail
Timor by ope*

Batavia

Coupang

Sunday Island

ENDEAVOUR STRAIT

AUSTRALIA

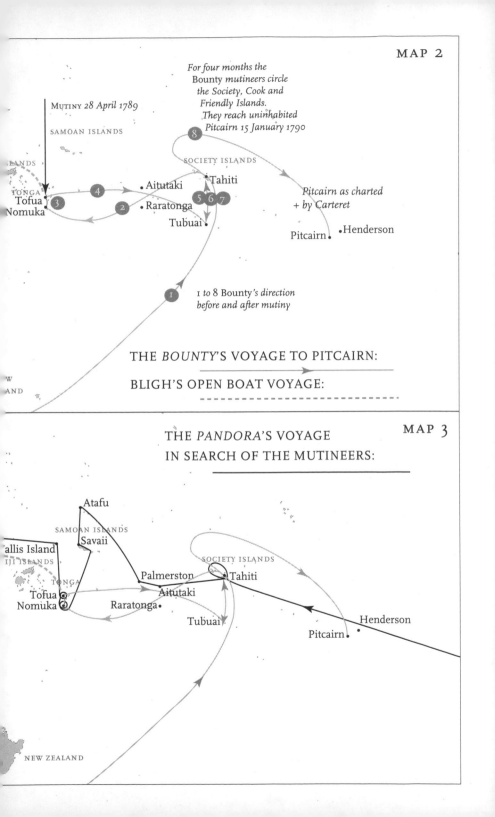

MAP 2

MUTINY 28 April 1789

For four months the
Bounty mutineers circle
the Society, Cook and
Friendly Islands.
They reach uninhabited
Pitcairn 15 January 1790

SAMOAN ISLANDS

⑧

SOCIETY ISLANDS

ISLANDS

·Aitutaki

·Tahiti

TONGA

④

⑤ ⑥ ⑦

Pitcairn as charted
+ by Carteret

Tofua ③

Nomuka

② ·Raratonga

Tubuai ·

·Henderson

Pitcairn·

①

1 to 8 Bounty's direction
before and after mutiny

THE *BOUNTY*'S VOYAGE TO PITCAIRN:

W

AND

BLIGH'S OPEN BOAT VOYAGE:

- -

MAP 3

THE *PANDORA*'S VOYAGE
IN SEARCH OF THE MUTINEERS:

Atafu

SAMOAN ISLANDS

Savaii

allis Island

IJI ISLANDS

SOCIETY ISLANDS

Palmerston ·Tahiti

TONGA

Tofua ⊚

Nomuka ⊚

Aitutaki

Raratonga·

Tubuai ·

Henderson

Pitcairn·

NEW ZEALAND

To the real Lady Myre

wherever she

now is

THE SWALLOWS ARE BACK – fewer than last year, fewer last year than the year before, four weeks of flying from Namibia, through the Congo rainforest, across the Sahara Desert, Morocco, eastern Spain and western France to here, their summer home.

The barn door is open. They nest in the same crumbling corners, use the same old nail as a joist, appraise the stream from an overhead phone wire. They wheel and feed. I wonder at their journey without maps, their composite soul, their timing. Year on year they return in this last week of April when the verges shimmer with bluebells.

I view them from my window. I too have returned. In this tumbledown mill cottage I try to make sense, from maps, of the journeys ships and boats have made. The voyage of the *Bounty* from Spithead to Tahiti on what might have been an unremarkable commercial venture. Its meandering from Tofua to Pitcairn Island after Fletcher Christian mutinied and hijacked it. William Bligh's extraordinary 3600 mile journey, cast adrift by Christian in an open boat with eighteen men, across the Pacific to Timor in ferocious seas. The wreck on the Great Barrier Reef of the *Pandora*, sent to capture Christian and the other mutineers. My own voyage from Tauranga to Pitcairn in a cargo ship, the *Tundra Princess*, and then from Pitcairn to Mangareva in a small catamaran with a lone yachtsman and Lady Myre.

I spin the globe and search these place names: specks of human reference of no concern to swallows. I view the coded world, see swathes of ocean, shapes of continents, islands. My journey has receded to fragments and shards of memory. I settle to the virtual reality of a computer screen, to pencilled notes and digital images. Only at uncertain times does a lament from mother or a faraway call from Lady Myre define my isolation, or a dream of true storm threaten my comfort.

I

ROSIE'S BLOUSE

Time is what stops everything from happening at once

1

On Monday 27 April 1789 Fletcher Christian, master's mate on the *Bounty*, held dawn watch from four to eight. A serene view of the sun rising over the Pacific Ocean belied the trouble that would change his life that day. The ship, like a floating garden, was sailing from Tahiti to the West Indies with a cargo of over a thousand breadfruit plants. Some were more than seven feet high. Sunlight illuminated a coral reef, atolls and white beaches. Christian took a green coconut from the heap piled on the quarterdeck, cracked it open and drank its watery milk. He thought this an act of 'no consequence', as insignificant as the flutter of a butterfly's wings.

Had he not taken that coconut I would not have trudged round Harrods on a June day 295 years later, looking for a blouse for his great-great-great-granddaughter Rosie. I was to stay with Rosie and her husband Hank on Pitcairn Island, if a ship would take me there. By email I'd asked if she'd like me to bring anything from London. 'Not really,' she replied. 'Just concentrate on getting here.' Then she described, if I happened to chance on it, a top to go with her pants, as she called them, a top that was dark, silky, size sixteen, wouldn't crease or show the dirt, pull-on not buttoned, low cut, nipped in below the bust, wide over the waist and hips...

The escalators heaved. I looked at garments made in Taiwan and China. I considered tops by Paul and Joe, and Sonia

Rykiel's pearl-encrusted jackets. Seeking the Way Out I passed hats that looked like hothouse plants. In Bridal Wear a cordoned-off bottle-blonded Sloane, swathed in cream silk, rehearsed her once-in-a-lifetime day.

I found Rosie's blouse in Fenwicks, made in Paris by Gerard Darel, £129, crushed silk, silver with charcoal blodges, size eighteen, loose sleeves, a low V-neck... Aviva, the ample Israeli assistant, said these were American sizes and came up small. She had this blouse herself: it washed well, needed no ironing, was a wonderful gift and truly flattering.

2

The day before the mutiny, the *Bounty* anchored to get supplies at Nomuka Island in the Tongan archipelago 1300 miles west of Tahiti. William Bligh bartered for coconuts – he settled at a price of twenty for a nail. He told Christian to take a boat and muskets, supervise casking water from the river and be watchful. The Nomukans were impoverished and hostile, they had sores on their bodies and suspicion in their eyes.

At the river's edge Christian was stoned and the boat's anchor stolen. He retreated to the ship. Bligh called him a coward and taunted him that he was armed and the islanders naked. Against the return of the anchor he took two chiefs hostage and held them on the *Bounty* until sunset. They beat themselves with their fists and wept with fear, but the anchor was gone, nothing was gained, and Christian above everyone was humiliated.

Bligh was rated as lieutenant of the *Bounty*, the smallness of the ship precluded a higher rank, but he acted as its captain and purser. He kept tight control of all supplies. The following morning when he went to the quarterdeck he thought his coconut pile was smaller. The master John Fryer said it looked that way only because men had walked over it in the night. Bligh didn't believe him. Enraged he summoned Christian, again berated him, said, 'Damn your blood, you've stolen my coconuts,' and called him a thief, a hell-hound and a beast.

Christian asked, 'Why do you treat me thus, Captain Bligh?'

'No reply,' said Bligh, then ordered the quartermasters to bring every coconut on the ship to the quarterdeck. He assembled the crew, told them, 'There never were such a set of damned thieving rascals under any man's command in the world before,' halved their daily supply of yams and vowed when the ship reached the Endeavour Strait he'd kill half of them, force the others to eat grass like cows, and make the officers jump overboard.

It was not a happy day aboard the *Bounty*. That afternoon Bligh again cursed Christian and called him a damned rascal and an infamous wretch. Christian cracked. He ran off crying. None of the crew had seen him cry before. 'Tears were running from his eyes in big drops,' William Purcell the carpenter said. 'Flesh and blood can't bear this,' Christian told him. 'I'd rather die ten thousand deaths. I always do my duty as an officer and a man, yet I receive this scandalous treatment.' Purcell tried to console him that the voyage home to England would not take long. Christian said, 'In going through the Endeavour Strait I am sure the ship will be in hell.'

Bligh's outbursts were part of his command. After them he

behaved as if nothing had happened. Purcell asked Christian why he took this incident so badly. Christian replied, 'Can you ask me and hear the treatment I receive?' Purcell said, 'Don't I receive as bad as you do?' Christian replied, 'You have your warrant to protect you so you can answer him. But if I should speak to him as you do, he would break me, turn me before the mast and flog me, and if he did, it would be the death of us both, for I'm sure I'd take him in my arms and jump overboard with him.'

Christian resolved to jump ship that night. He lashed together two masts to form a makeshift raft, packed bread, fruit and pork in a clothes bag, took nails to use as barter and gave away his Tahitian souvenirs: his carved wooden figures, black pearls and drum made of sharkskin. He intended to slip from the side of the ship in the dark and float on this makeshift raft until local Polynesians in their canoes saw him. He'd bribe them with nails to take him to a shore, then make his way back to Tahiti.

His plan was thwarted. A volcano on the island of Tofua erupted as the *Bounty* passed in the dark. The crew gathered on deck to wonder as magma and flames spurted to the sky. They thought they were viewing the wrath of God. For Christian it was an obstacle to his escape from his tormentor.

He didn't sleep. He plotted with Matthew Quintal a Cornish seaman, and the gunner's mate John Mills. Quintal got the key to the arms store on the pretext that he needed a gun to shoot a shark that was following the ship. At dawn the three men burst into Bligh's cabin, said they'd kill him if he made a noise, pushed him to his stomach, tied back his hands, hauled him out of bed, dragged him in his nightshirt to the mizzen mast, swore at him as he had sworn at them and warned they'd blow his brains out if he tried to resist.

Of the crew of forty-five men, twenty joined in or were implicated in the fracas of Christian's mutiny. Quintal and other armed men guarded the hatches and the officers' cabins. Christian held a musket to Bligh's head and shouted orders. He made the boatswain William Cole lower the ship's launch, then ordered him and eighteen other Bligh 'loyalists' into this open boat: John Smith Bligh's personal servant, John Fryer the master, William Elphinstone the master's mate, the gunner, the carpenter, the acting surgeon, three midshipmen, two quartermasters, the quartermaster's mate, the sailmaker, the master-at-arms, the cook, the butcher and David Nelson the gardener, who grieved to be separated from the 1114 breadfruit plants he'd potted and nurtured in Tahiti.

In a scene of violence, panic and surprise these men struggled to get supplies for survival into the boat: twine, canvas, sails, a twenty-eight-gallon cask of water. William Purcell took his tool chest, John Smith got a hundred and fifty pounds of bread, six bottles of wine, six quarts of rum, a quadrant-compass, Bligh's journals and commission and some of the ship's papers. Christian said he'd kill him if he touched any of Bligh's collection over fifteen years of maps, astronomical observations, surveys and drawings, or his sextant or time-keeper.

Christian then told Bligh, 'Your officers and men are in the boat and you must go with them. Attempt the least resistance and you'll instantly be put to death.' Then he shoved him down the Jacob's ladder at gunpoint.

The launch measured twenty-three feet long, six feet nine inches wide and two feet nine inches deep. The men's weight sank it to the surface of the sea. The mutineers veered it astern with a rope, chucked in sixteen bits of pork and four cutlasses, jeered at Bligh and his crew, then cast them adrift on the open ocean.

3

Aviva wrapped Rosie's top in layers of tissue paper. It would take up little space in my Eagle Creek bag. She was interested in my intention to visit Pitcairn Island, for she'd seen three film versions of *Mutiny on the Bounty* and once glimpsed Marlon Brando in a Florida store.

I told her of the island's remoteness, how difficult it was to get there because ships seldom stopped and it had no airstrip, how its small population was descended from Fletcher Christian and other *Bounty* mutineers and the Tahitian women they'd abducted, how some of the men who now lived there had committed serious sexual crimes, how there was no bank, shops, cars, television, hotel or anything much except coconut palms and the pounding surf.

She asked if my husband was travelling with me. There was a pause. I told her I wanted to write a book about Pitcairn. She asked if I'd had anything published. Again I deflected. I talked of my interest in tangential associations, such as how a woman sneezing in China can cause a snowstorm in Alaska, or how Fletcher Christian taking a coconut could transform my life. I expounded on the ramifications of a chance event and how these affected a narrative. Reality, I told her, was not stable but full of disorder, confusion, and change. She looked apprehensively for the next customer, said she hoped I'd enjoy my adventure and that Rosie would like her lovely blouse and that she thought Mel Gibson much better as Fletcher Christian than Marlon Brando, because Brando wasn't quite a man, if I knew what she meant.

I took my present home on the 23 bus.

Verity liked the top but couldn't envisage when Rosie would wear it on Pitcairn. I said perhaps at Christmas or for church on Saturdays. Saturday became the Pitcairners' Sabbath after they were converted to Seventh Day Adventism by American evangelists from the Napa Valley in 1876. 'You have', Verity said, 'a confused idea of the journey you hope to make.'

I agreed. She boiled spaghetti and chopped broccoli and I spoke of a fractured world. I said that to go on a real journey was to face danger and surprise, and that only in the virtual worlds to which we now retreated was a false security assured. Verity looked uncomfortable. Some people who have descriptive names inform life's narrative with them. Among the *Bounty* crew Robert Lamb was the butcher. In my quest for flexible flights to the southern hemisphere I was being advised by Harold Wing. That Verity's second name was Lord, perhaps influenced her to deal in certainties. She kept a crucifix in her trinket box and found consolation for all horror in the liturgy of the Catholic Church.

9

I tried to be lighter. Didn't she find it strange, I asked, the language Fletcher Christian used to William Purcell the carpenter, about his relationship with William Bligh – when he said if Bligh flogged him he'd take him in his arms and jump overboard with him. Didn't she find that a disturbing sexual image, a fantasy of fatal bonding? It wasn't that he'd shoot Bligh, shove him in the sea, then sail off with the ship: he'd take him in his arms, jump overboard with him and hold him until the tide overwhelmed them both. To me, I said, it sounded like a lovers' tragedy not a mutineer's triumph.

Verity grated the Parmesan and said she wished I'd talk about something else. I persisted. Did she not think it probable, I asked, that Bligh buggered Christian nightly and that was what the coconut business was all about: sado-masochistic sex?

I knew she was worse than irritated because the bridge of her nose had gone white. I said that a triviality was like a pinprick spy hole into chaos, that a fire might smoulder for a long time, then a chance puff of wind would make it rage, that I thought the tattoos on Christian's arse and heart were for Bligh, that it was wrong of Bligh to call him a thief in front of the ship's crew, that on Tahiti, when Bligh wanted to be revered by Otoo the chief, he said Christian wasn't a friend – his friend, he said, was King George the Third.

'Please!' said Verity emphatically. So we talked of other things: how long the summer nights now were, and how swiftly the year had passed. Then she said she had something important to tell me and I felt a prescience, a foreboding. She said two days ago it had been her birthday and I'd forgotten this, not even given her a card. That of itself, she said, was perhaps of no great importance but it seemed indicative of how estranged we'd become.

I apologised. As recompense, I asked if she'd like to go with me the following day to the National Maritime Museum to see the *Bounty* artefacts on display. I suggested we go by passenger ferry down the Thames from Millbank Pier, and when we returned I'd buy her lunch in the Oxo Tower. She made an exasperated noise, a sort of whistle and click of her teeth, and said she was meeting a friend.

Later in my room, as I rewrapped Rosie's blouse in its tissue paper, I mused on Verity's rebuke. Perhaps it was true that I'd become so immersed in scenes from the past and plans for the future that I'd lost my connection to the present. Verity was given to citing biblical exhortations about the sufficiency of the day. I put Rosie's blouse with my travel things and read a page of notes for my book:

Pitcairn Island is an isolated lump of craggy inhospitable rock 5 miles in diameter in the middle of the Pacific Ocean 2500 miles north-east of New Zealand at latitude 25° 0.4 mins south and longitude 30° 0.5 mins west. In 2004 it had a permanent population of 49 people, seven of whom were men charged under British law with rape and serious sexual abuse of underage girls. Other species include unnumbered rats, mice, feral cats, wild fowl, land crabs, hawks, petrels, noddy, booby and bosum birds. There are short-tailed albatrosses, cahows and dark-rumped petrels, humpback and blue whales, green sea and loggerhead turtles and bright-coloured parrot fish. There is one giant turtle called Mr, or perhaps Mrs, Turpen. Two such turtles were brought from the Galapagos Islands in 1955 but one was shot by a boy, as was a lone baby seal that tried sunning itself on the shore. The rocks round Pitcairn have not been colonised by seals.

A phone call from mother interrupted my efforts: her usual despairing lament. A phantom vandal with a key to her house had scratched the furniture and torn the lampshades. This phantom visited nightly. Sometimes she – for the culprit was a woman – did useful things like regrouting the bathroom tiles or changing the light bulbs, but mostly she destroyed. She smeared woodstain on the Davenport, tarnished the silver, picked holes in the silk rugs and stole knickers and scarves. I enquired why anyone should want to do such pointless things. Ask her, was my mother's reply.

I supposed that many of those on the *Bounty* had sailed to the South Seas to escape the exigencies of home: debts, disaffected wives and girlfriends, paranoid mothers, failures and disappointments.

In bed that night Verity turned her back, so letting me know we were not to be entwined in sleep or the familiarity of what I'd thought to be love. I took her to be saying: Go your way, make your stupid journey and leave me free to live my life.

I lay awake and thought about forgetfulness. If I went away I'd forget Verity. She'd shift to a recess of my mind, a trace element, like most of the books I'd ever read, like most of the lovers I'd ever had, a residual memory, a vague disquiet. Things had become distant between us, so why should I stay? I thought of my mother's insane forgetfulness, confusion and strange inventions. And then I remembered with pain a night of Verity's face so close to mine on the pillow, our kisses like cool clear water, our whispered caresses, the call of barn owls in the moonlight, but not the owls in the barn at Mill Cottage – another barn another pillow. I felt regretful about separating from her and spooned her body to me in an echo of our familiar loving ways.

The ferry to Greenwich from Bankside was a trippers' bus, a soulless glass-encased catamaran. A guide gave a worn-out commentary: 'To your left Christopher Wren's monument shaped like a candle. To your right HMS *Belfast*. That's the Anchor public house. That's the Globe Theatre.' I wished Verity were with me and that we'd packed egg sandwiches and a Thermos of tea.

There was one glass case of *Bounty* artefacts on show at the Maritime Museum. The model of the ship was small but exact. It showed the complex rigging, Bligh's cabin, the ventilation grilles for the breadfruit plants and the windows to give them light. I saw the relative smallness of the open launch in which Bligh made his journey from Tofua to Timor, without charts, across the great South Sea.

There was a polished coconut shell engraved by him with 'the cup I eat my miserable allowance out of. 28 April 1789'. There was the tiny horn beaker with which he rationed drinking water for each man three times a day, one of the bullets he used to weigh their morsels of bread, his clay pipe, his little silver corkscrew, magnifying glass and reading glass. There was a facsimile of Robert Dodd's 1790 painting of 'The mutineers turning Lieutenant Bligh and part of the officers and crew adrift from His Majesty's ship the *Bounty*', and an engraving of Bligh by John Condé, done in 1792 from a portrait by John Russell. It showed a feminine face with Cupid's bow lips, bright eyes and an intelligent brow – I wondered if it was a fusspot face and if cruelty was discernible.

I pondered the gap between the souvenirs of the museum and the violence of the ocean, between description and the thing itself, between a frozen portrait and a living face and between life and its reflection in glass.

4

Bligh, when he sailed from England to Tahiti, left behind Elizabeth his toothy, plump, round-faced wife, and three daughters: Harriet, Mary, Betsy and a fourth, Fanny, on the way.

Fletcher Christian was twenty-three, ten years younger than Bligh and unmarried. He was five feet nine, with dark skin and hair, muscled arms and bow legs. He sweated a lot, had a sticky handshake and liked to show off – turning somersaults, lifting heavy things and balancing a gun on the palm of his hand.

Born in Cockermouth in Cumberland, a market town with mills and coalmines, fertile valleys and wooded hills, he was the fifth and last surviving child. Fletcher was his maternal grandmother's family name. When he was three his father died. His mother paid for her elder sons to read law and medicine at Cambridge but got into debt, and by 1780, when she was thirty-eight, owed £6500. To avoid the debtors' gaol she moved to the port of Douglas on the Isle of Man. Bligh was living there, back from a four-year voyage of exploration to the

South Seas as Captain Cook's sailing master on HMS *Resolution*. He'd seen Cook murdered and hacked to pieces in Kealakekua Bay in Hawaii by hostile islanders – a murder that made him aggressively vigilant in his own command.

Without money for an education, Fletcher Christian joined the navy aged seventeen. He liked naval life. 'It is very easy to make one's self beloved and respected on board ship,' he wrote to his brother Charles. 'One has only to be always ready to obey one's superior officers and to be kind to the common man.' On a two-year voyage to India, on the merchant ship HMS *Eurydice*, he was promoted to acting lieutenant and watch leader. In 1785 he wrote to Bligh asking if he'd take him as midshipman on a voyage Bligh was to captain to the West Indies. Bligh had his full complement of men so turned him down. Christian persisted – said he'd work for no pay and wanted only to learn his profession from a navigator as respected as Bligh.

They made two voyages together before the catastrophe of the *Bounty*. Christian became Bligh's protégé, favoured and tutored by him. He dined with him on board ship, was a guest at his house and a family friend. Bligh asked to have him as his midshipman on the *Bounty*. Christian held him in intense regard. He described him as 'very passionate'. Bligh was his surrogate father, his role model.

Something happened to warp his respect and good feelings. Charles, when he heard of the mutiny, thought only extreme provocation could have made Fletcher act so out of character. He said he was 'slow to be moved'. He wondered if it was the stress of proximity:

When men are cooped up for a long Time in the Interior of a Ship there oft prevails such jarring Discordancy of Tempers and Conduct that it is enough on many Occasions by repeated Acts of Irritation and Offence to change the Disposition of a Lamb into That of an Animal Fierce and Resentful.

But on that aborted journey from Tahiti to the West Indies, Christian was cooped up in the *Bounty* interior for only three weeks before he mutinied. He'd lived for five indulgent months on Tahiti. No one spoke of him as an angry man, he was disposed to be obedient and kind. The 'jarring Discordancy' was provoked by Bligh's erosion of trust and accumulation of insult. It turned Christian's love of him to hate.

5

It wasn't easy for me to get to Pitcairn in 2004. Press reports of the depraved behaviour of Fletcher Christian's descendants, and criminal charges for their crimes against girls – gang rape, serial rape, gross indecency – made the islanders wary of visits from strangers. And this tiny isolated island, this remote, unwanted British dependency, had no transport links with anywhere. Most islands in the South Pacific, administered by the French, had airstrips and ferry links. But not Pitcairn.

There was satellite email, though – set up for the judges and lawyers who'd go from Auckland, in a boat chartered by the British government, to conduct the trials. Islanders too could log on for free, though there was no privacy to their mail. Rosie advised my best chance was to travel with Graham

Wragg Expeditions from the island of Mangareva, 300 miles east of Pitcairn, which had an air link with Tahiti. Wragg, a New Zealand botanist, was chartered by the French Polynesian authorities to sail his catamaran *Bounty Bay* through their waters to Pitcairn. I emailed him. He said he'd take me. A cost of thirteen hundred US dollars would include two days on the uninhabited island of Henderson, 107 miles east-north-east of Pitcairn, where I might see the Ridley turtle, the dark-rumped petrel and the flightless rail. I was to meet him on the quay at Rikitea, Mangareva's only settlement.

I paid the money into his Oxford account and rebooked my flights with Harold Wing. 'Welcome aboard *Bounty Bay*,' Wragg wrote. He recommended the Tahiti Airport Lodge, 'Clean and friendly, five minutes up the hill from the airport.' He said he'd sort a *pension* on Mangareva, advised me to bring sunburn cream and seasickness pills and wrote of a fantastic tour into the centre of Tahiti to the crater of the volcano from which the island was born.

Rosie said bring something nice to wear for church, but apart from that just shorts, jeans and maybe a fleece because it was cool in the evenings. There were mosquitoes, I'd need repellent, and did I eat special food? She added a caution. Things to do with Pitcairn seldom worked out as planned. Shipping was unreliable and dependent on the weather. It was a fact of life. They were used to it.

Within a week came an email from Wragg. I deserved a medal for perseverance but he had 'frustrating' news. There'd been a change of government in Tahiti, his permission to sail in French waters was under review, voyages to Pitcairn were on hold, it was all a mess, he was trying to sort it, it would take him months. 'Hope your air tickets are date changeable. Sorry about this.' Startled questions from me were blocked by auto-reply. Wragg and the *Bounty Bay* were at sea.

Two weeks later he emailed that he couldn't risk having his boat impounded by the Tahitian authorities. It had happened before and cost him twenty thousand US dollars in fines. The new Tahitian president, Oscar Temaru, was pro-Polynesian independence and had a one-seat majority over the outgoing pro-France man Gaston Flosse, whose staff had all been sacked and taken their paperwork with them. The British authorities didn't want outsiders on Pitcairn while the sex trials were going on, and the Pitcairn governor had asked him not to rock the boat – his boat – with the French Polynesian authorities at this delicate time. Maybe he'd be able to take me next year, but trials and international manoeuvrings between governments were way above anything he could influence. I wondered about the reimbursement of my thirteen hundred dollars.

6

The whole *Bounty* endeavour was a 'jarring Discordancy' to Bligh. Even before setting off from Spithead he was frustrated and bad-tempered.

His commission was to take the breadfruit saplings acquired in Tahiti to the West Indies to form plantations to feed the colony's starving slaves. He was to sail via the

Endeavour Strait so as to chart that stretch of ocean which was little known and dangerous.

The architect of the enterprise, Sir Joseph Banks, botanical adviser to King George the Third, traveller and rich entrepreneur, had recommended Bligh to the Admiralty. He thought him a brilliant navigator. They'd sailed together to Tahiti with Captain Cook, so Banks knew Bligh was on good terms with the island's chiefs. But the Admiralty, preoccupied with war in Europe, gave scant attention to this commercial voyage of a small ship and Bligh was demeaned by a commission which didn't even merit the official rank of captain and which gave him only a lieutenant's pay.

He supervised the transformation of the *Bethia*, a merchant ship eighty-five feet long and rated only as a cutter, into the *Bounty*. He turned the great cabin into a conservatory for the saplings, with skylights, air vents and a lead floor cut with hundreds of holes, each fitted with a pot and drainage pipe. His private cabin was a windowless annexe. He was meticulous over detail and the Admiralty was slow to respond to all his queries, so the ship wasn't ready until October, months later than he'd expected. He worried about setting off late and rounding the notorious Cape Horn in bad weather. Then, when there was a fine fair wind, he remained stuck at Spithead for three weeks because the Admiralty failed to give clearance to sail. The weather worsened, gales swept the Channel and the dispirited crew suffered colds and rheumatism. Bligh wanted the Admiralty bureaucrats punished for negligence.

While they waited, Fletcher Christian met up with his

brother Charles, back from a voyage to India on which he'd served as ship's surgeon. At the start of it, Charles said, he'd been full of life and vigour, 'like a tree in promising blossom', but he'd returned blighted, disappointed and ill. And he was to be charged with involvement in mutiny, a charge that led to a two-year suspension from the navy. Perhaps he communicated mutinous disaffection to Fletcher.

Bligh, disappointed from the start, set sail on 23 December 1787 in rough, stormy weather. Such late departure meant he reached the hazards of Cape Horn towards the end of March – entirely the wrong time for safe passage round that perilous stretch of ocean where gales and waves up to sixty-five feet high prevailed for all but thirty days of the year.

It was a voyage of missed winds and lost opportunities. Within hours of leaving Spithead, in rough seas a man was injured in a fall from the mainsail. For three days waves broke over the ship and washed away beer casks, spare yards and spars, loosened the three boats* and ruined the bread. 'We were an entire Sea on Deck,' Bligh wrote in his log. He was critical of the design of the ship and its small size and thought the complement of forty-five men too few and their calibre poor.

On the voyage out to Tahiti, Christian was his prize pupil, good-mannered and keen to please. Bligh made him acting lieutenant, assigned him morning watch, dined with him and even loaned him money despite his own modest pay. When they stopped at Tenerife it was Christian he sent as his envoy

* A launch of 23 feet, a cutter of 18 feet and a jolly boat of 16 feet.

to negotiate with the governor for supplies of beef, pumpkins, potatoes and wood.

Bligh's vigilance was constant. He was assiduous in keeping his crew healthy, disciplined and fed. When rain and humidity caused mildew, he had the ship aired with fires and sprinkled with vinegar. In clear weather he saw that all hatchways were opened and bedding and clothes washed. Drinking water was filtered through dripstones. Cooped seabirds were force-fed with corn so they didn't taste fishy. He made sure all men had sufficient rest, that they ate sauerkraut to ward off scurvy, and hot porridge for breakfast when nights were cold. After Sunday inspection for cleanliness he held 'Divine Service'. But his rigid discipline and efficiency were untempered by tact. He was high-handed, quick to anger, and worse than caustic. He chided one man in front of another, jeered if they made mistakes and made them feel like fools. He didn't disguise his disdain for his crew and complained often to them about the absence of trained marines and commissioned officers.

Every afternoon from five to eight he made them all dance, 'for Relaxation and Mirth', to the music of Michael Byrne, the ship's near-blind violinist. He thought this conducive to health. When John Mills the gunner's mate, and William Brown the assistant gardener, refused to comply with such obligatory fun, Bligh stopped their grog. He judged Matthew Quintal insolent and mutinous, so had him stripped to the waist, bound by his wrists and watched by the crew while he was lashed two dozen times. He fell out with John Fryer the master, and with the surgeon Thomas Huggan. Both refused to dine with him. Bligh called Huggan, with reason, a fat, lazy, entirely incompetent sot and noted in his log that he was constantly drunk. (Huggan diagnosed scurvy when William Brown complained of rheumatism, James Valentine, an able seaman, died of an infection after being 'bled' by him for some minor ailment, and he described his own delirium tremens as caused by 'paralytic affection'.)

After three months, on 28 March 1788, the *Bounty* reached Cape Horn. For twenty-five days Bligh forced the ship against great waves, gales and driving winds, snow, sleet and hail. The decks flooded, men were injured trying to manage the sails, eight became ill with exhaustion, the cook broke a rib, Huggan dislocated his shoulder. When neither men nor ship could take any more, Bligh turned and headed east to approach Tahiti via the Cape of Good Hope, southern Australia and New Zealand. By this change he added ten thousand miles to the journey. From Spithead to Tahiti he logged twenty-eight thousand miles. He arrived in October 1788. The voyage had taken ten months. Bligh prided himself on having kept all but one of his crew alive in extreme conditions. But the men had had enough of him. William Purcell said he watched them solely to find fault.

7

The Tahitians had cause to be chary about visits from English mariners. Twenty years before the *Bounty* saga, on 18 June 1767, the *Dolphin* arrived at the island captained by Samuel Wallis, a Cornishman. His commission by the Admiralty was

'To discover and obtain a complete knowledge of the Land or Islands supposed to be situated in the Southern Hemisphere'. When he reached Tahiti and saw mountains obscured by cloud he thought he'd discovered 'the Southern Continent'.

The islanders, intrigued as his ship came into view, paddled out to it in their canoes. As a symbol of peace and friendship they held up plantain branches and at Wallis's invitation they surged on board ship to marvel at this floating island. In the noise and excitement a goat butted one of them on the bottom. The man turned, saw a creature 'so different from any he had ever seen' rearing on its hind legs to butt him again. In terror he jumped overboard. Screaming, other Tahitians jumped too or scrambled to their canoes. This was no friendly ship. It housed monsters.

Wallis had been months at sea and needed water and fresh food. He sent a boat to the shore. It was stoned by tribesmen. As a warning, he fired a nine-pound cannon ball across the water and his commanding officer, Lieutenant Furneaux, fired buckshot at the stone throwers, wounding one of them in the shoulder. In search of safe anchorage Wallis then sailed to another part of the island. Again he tried to send a boat to the shore, again islanders threatened it with clubs and paddles, and again Wallis's men fired. They killed one man and grievously wounded another.

There was a day's silence, then a few Tahitians approached the ship in canoes. They bartered hogs, fowl and fruit, for nails, knives and trinkets. But then two thousand of them paddled out in three hundred canoes and circled round. Women made alluring gestures to the *Dolphin*'s crew, men sang, blew conches and played flutes. From a canopied canoe a chief handed up a bunch of red and yellow feathers for Wallis, while large canoes filled with men converged. Another chief held up a coconut-tree branch. There was a 'Universal Shout' and the men in the canoes showered the *Dolphin* with stones. Again Wallis ordered fire. He sprayed small shot indiscriminately at the Tahitians, who panicked, retreated, then reconverged. Wallis fired the ship's great guns. The canoes scattered, regrouped, hoisted white streamers, and tribesmen armed with slings hurled two-pound stones at the ship.

Wallis smashed the force of the ship's cannon at the islanders until they fled from the sea and into the forest. Next morning a party of English sailors landed in Matavai Bay. It was deserted. Close to the river's estuary Lieutenant Furneaux stuck a British flag into the ground and in the name of His Majesty declared this land King George the Third's Island.

A dozen Tahitians paddled out to the ship and in supplication offered gifts of hogs and green plantain leaves and made a speech which was not understood. Unchallenged, Wallis sent boats to the shore for water. When the islanders again dared approach the ship in canoes filled with stones, he ordered tremendous fire from all the ship's guns. He bombarded the canoes, the woods, the hills where the women and children were hiding. Within minutes no creature was to be seen. He then sent armed boats to destroy all the moored canoes. Many were sixty feet long and had taken years of painstaking work to build.

Defeated, the Tahitians gave the English all they wanted: water, hogs, sex, fruit, vegetables. In exchange they were given nails, bits of iron and beads. A woman was brought to the cutter where this barter was taking place. Two men had to support her, for she kept collapsing. She stared in wonder at the English strangers, then wept. Her husband and three of her sons had been killed by their gunfire. She shook Wallis's hand and gave him two hogs but would accept nothing from him in return.

8

Because supply ships called so rarely at Pitcairn and there were no shops, I wanted the blouse I'd bought in London to be a memorable present, stylish and special. Bligh, when he sailed to Tahiti, took cheap gifts to buy favours – a hundred pounds of glass beads, 168 mirrors, 72 shirts. But he knew that above all else the islanders wanted iron, for they had none of their own. 'For traffic with the natives' he took 1000 lbs of nails, 576 cheap knives, 2808 custom-made axes and boxes of saws, drills and files.

All that the Tahitians made came from their island. Their most effective armament was a slingshot of plaited coconut fibre, filled with stones and swung with terrific force round their heads. They made clubs, lances and spears from wood and shell, chisels from bone, nails from wood, needles from bamboo or fishbone and hammers and anchors from stone. They used conch shells as megaphones and built ocean-going boats from trees hollowed to hulls and joined by transverse beams. The largest of these accommodated 150 paddlers, surpassed any western boat for speed, and could withstand the most violent seas.

They fished at night by moonlight, their canoes illuminated by candle-nuts,* with lines made from coconut fibre and hooks of mother-of-pearl. They used the glittering hooks as artificial flies without bait. In the reefs they speared fish with sharpened bamboo. If they caught a large fish they hauled it with ropes from the sterns of the canoes on to an outrigger.

When weird-looking sailors arrived from nowhere in a magnificent floating town, they saw at first encounter how transforming iron might be. On his visit in the *Dolphin,* Wallis described a test he devised. He laid out a *Johannes* (a twenty-two-carat gold coin), a golden guinea, a silver crown, a Spanish dollar, a few shillings, some brass halfpennies, and two large nails, then invited the Tahitians to choose. They always took the nails first, then the halfpennies. They had no particular interest in the other coins. 'Their thirst after iron is irresistible,' he wrote. His crew then stripped the ship of its nails because they could buy any imaginable sexual favour for the price of a nail. 'The men even drew out of different parts of the ship those nails that fastened the cleats† to her side.'

Bligh, in return for nails, wanted a thousand breadfruit plants from the Tahitians, he didn't tell them why. His crew, like Wallis's, wanted every imaginable sexual favour, as well as fresh water, wood, fruit, fish and hospitality in the sunshine. I, with my blouse for Rosie, signalled my desire for friendship with her in the hope she'd treat me well.

---

* The kernels of spurgewort, *Aleurites triloba,* the candleberry tree.
† Wedges of wood for securing ropes etc.

9

On Tahiti Bligh was the celebrity guest, the visiting dignitary, bearing gifts from an unimagined land. He called the island 'The Paradise of the World' and said he'd travelled far but found nowhere more beautiful. Chief Otoo fêted him with great goodwill and rejoicing and gave him hogs, breadfruit, fish, capsicums, pumpkins and so many coconuts that none of the crew drank water any more. Otoo's wife and sister spread mats for him to recline on, draped him in their finest cloth, held his hands as they escorted him round the island and brought a picture of Captain Cook in a broken frame for him to repair.

Otoo asked if Christian was Bligh's *tyo* – his special friend. Bligh offended Christian by saying he wasn't, that King George the Third was his *tyo*. It was one offence of many. He convinced the Tahitians he was doing them a favour by taking their island's breadfruit as a present for his king. He warned the crew not to divulge the true purpose of the visit in case this increased the cost, nor were they to mention Cook's death for fear of creating unease.

Bligh wooed the Tahitians with nails and beads. 'They appeared extremely satisfied,' he wrote in his log. They also loved cast-off British clothes, would discard their clean, bright-coloured wraps for a dirty old English shirt, and were 'mad' for strong liquor and getting drunk on rum, brandy or wine. Bligh showed them the workings of the ship and they shouted with excitement when he fired the great guns across the sea. When they saw a swallow shot it was 'impossible to describe the pleasure they evinced'. They picked up the spent bullets in amazement. Bligh promised, when he next visited, to bring arms and ammunition from the king. To reciprocate, Otoo had two dresses made for George the Third.

Bligh was given permission to set up camp at Point Venus. Tahitians were barred from this area. Christian supervised the erecting of tents and a bamboo shed to house the saplings and made sure that sea shells were put in the base of the pots for drainage.

Because so many plants were wanted, Bligh, Nelson the gardener and a party of men went inland to the deep valley to persuade chiefs of different regions to give them trees. That his king should want a thousand breadfruit saplings was one of the many things the Tahitians found mystifying about Bligh. They asked bemused questions about the Christian god he spoke of. Did he come from the wind or the sun? Who was there before him? Who was the mother of his only son?

With reciprocal curiosity Bligh noted Tahitian customs in his log: how they bathed each morning in fresh-water streams, how small children were such adept swimmers they could pick up any tiny bead thrown into the water, how women often slept and ate in different houses from the men, and how the 'favours' of married women and of unmarried women of 'the better sort' were as hard to obtain as in any country. But he also wrote of parents who bargained 'the untasted charms of their child' for a couple of shirts and three strings of beads, of women who 'danced with their fore part Naked to the Company making many lewd gestures', of men who bound their penises with twine and stones to the sound of flute and drum music. He expressed surprise at the islanders' laughter at such displays.

The Tahitians lived on an island of plenty and in harmony with the sea. They built ocean-going boats bigger than the *Bounty*. Their diet was varied, their culture rich. They didn't need these visitors who brought viral infections and rats from their ship. Venereal disease was passed to them and in time children were born with it. Bligh's favoured lads, Fletcher Christian and Peter Heywood, who was sixteen, were treated for it by the egregious Dr Huggan. If Bligh was treated, it was not recorded.

The *Bounty* crew all found *tyos* and sexual partners. They bought sex with girls for beads or a shirt and anything for a nail. They got ornately tattooed and lived indulgently. But Bligh's temper didn't improve in this 'Paradise of the World'. He reacted savagely when things went wrong. He'd reached Tahiti in the monsoon season so he couldn't leave until the following April. It was difficult for him to control his crew on the island for nearly six months and he continued to view them as riff-raff. He called his petty officers neglectful and worthless and chided them for inefficiency and incompetence.

Anything unguarded on the ship and its boats, if deemed useful, was taken by the Tahitians. What was perceived by the English as pilfering was viewed differently by a society that shared material things. Bligh conceded that, 'were the ship lying in the river Thames a hundred times more would have been stolen'. Polynesians saw a distinction between casual pilfering and clever theft. Hiro, the god of thieving, inspired only the chosen with real skill.

Within days the *Bounty*'s best-bower anchor was taken, then the rudder, the gudgeon from the cutter and the butcher's cleaver. On Bligh's instruction the boat-keeper, Robert Lamb the butcher and William Muspratt the cook's assistant were then all lashed a dozen times for neglect of duty. The Tahitian women were shocked to witness these harsh punishments. Matthew Thompson was lashed for insolence and disobedience. William Purcell was confined to his cabin for refusing to make a whetstone. When a small Tahitian boy got injured as he helped haul the launch to the shore, Dr Huggan was too drunk to attend him. The boy survived, but Huggan died of alcohol poisoning. Bligh didn't grieve. Huggan, who spent most of his time in bed, had given capricious treatment for fanciful ailments – pneumoniotha or cholera morbus.

In the months on Tahiti Bligh's discipline eroded. The spare sails he'd wanted aired became mildewed, the ship's timepiece was left to run down, the azimuth compass was stolen. He said if he'd had anyone to replace the master and boatswain, 'they should no longer occupy their respective stations'.

Resentment among the crew festered then burst out. On 5 January 1789 Charles Churchill master-at-arms, and able seamen William Muspratt and John Millward, loaded the ship's cutter with guns and ammunition then sailed it to the bay. They intended to escape by canoe to the island of Tethuroa. Bligh let the Tahitians know that unless they were captured he'd 'make the whole country suffer for it'. Thomas Hayward, the officer on watch, was put in irons, and Bligh, armed with pocket pistols, went with a party of Tahitians to round up the deserters. He found them in a house five miles from the ship and the arms were retrieved, apart from a musket and two bayonets. Two lots of flogging followed: twelve lashes on each occasion for Churchill, twenty-four for Muspratt and Millward. They were kept in irons until their skin healed enough for the second round.

That same week Bligh gave the seaman Isaac Martin nineteen lashes for striking a Tahitian. A few days later the ship was almost wrecked when it ran aground. Then someone almost severed the anchor cable. Had they succeeded, the ship would have foundered on the reef. The vehemence of Bligh's anger alarmed the Tahitians. Otoo was mystified by it, his wife Iddeah wept and his parents left for the mountains even though it was raining heavily.

Bligh had a platform built in the fo'c'sle for a sentinel to guard the cable night and day. He suspected sabotage, as a ploy for his men to stay on Tahiti. Vanity barred him from thinking they might be tired of his rages and punishments. Hayward's *tyo* was implicated. He was thought to be vengeful of the punishment meted to his friend, or at least to have agreed to do the deed for him. He was given a hundred lashes, his back swelled and the skin broke. He was put in irons but escaped and dived overboard.

On Friday 27 January the gardener began to load the breadfruit plants into the *Bounty* conservatory. Roots were pushing through the containers. There were 774 pots, thirty-nine tubs, and twenty-four boxes of saplings. There were also exotic Tahitian specimens for Joseph Banks's botanical collection at

Kew: the chestnut-like *rata, peeah* which the Tahitians ate as a pudding, *ettow* and *matte* which gave them a red dye, and the *oraiah,* a sort of plantain. Bligh and the crew were given leaving presents: wooden carvings, musical instruments, black pearls and cloth. Otoo wanted to be saluted with the great guns as the *Bounty* pulled out to sea, but Bligh was afraid this would disturb the plants. Instead, he ordered all the men to gather on deck and give three cheers for Tahiti as the ship sailed from the bay.

10

Verity stayed with friends. The rooms we'd shared looked empty. We were polite when we met, but politeness seemed like proof of distance. One evening she mooted her plan to move to a provincial town, and asked if I'd keep this place on or go to Mill Cottage until I decided what I wanted. I thought of Bligh's contention that his crew had no attachments in their home country, so they mutinied to stay on Tahiti.

I talked of my problems in getting to Pitcairn Island. 'This is the twenty-first century,' Verity said. 'If you want to go anywhere on the planet you buy a ticket then get on a plane, train, ship or bus.' I said Pitcairn was not like that. 'But why go there anyway?' she asked and not for the first time. 'There's enough about Pitcairn on the net and in the news. Why choose somewhere so weird and far away?' I said it was a question of living connections, of being dissatisfied with virtual reality, of letting the real world impinge. I again expounded on random correlations that challenge ideas of linear narrative, predetermina-

tion or contiguousness. I told her how, in a deterministic system, later states evolve from earlier ones according to a fixed
law, whereas in a random system the move from earlier to
later states is not determined by any law. She gave me an
appraising stare and said that in her view love was a fixed connection and that narrative without it was bleak. As for life as a
series of random happenings, that was OK if I didn't mind
loneliness and loss.

I reflected on this alone in my room. I feared I'd sounded
pretentious. It was my choice to go to Pitcairn. It was not
essential. Verity's view of life was directional whereas I shook
all the bits, like in a kaleidoscope, to see how they'd arrange
themselves next. I wondered if I was as mutinous and impul-
sive as Fletcher Christian, scuppering the ordinary unmomen-
tous journey that might have been my life because of some
reckless dissatisfaction or need to subvert.

Self-doubt wasn't helped by a call from mother. She'd
sacked Wendy the latest Country Cousin, and the phantom
persecutor had painted her red azalea pink and left a single
footprint in the bath. She'd been to the police. She intended to
barricade herself in the house with a poker to hand to bludg-
eon the assailant when next she appeared. I felt the chaos of
her irrational universe and in a troubled dream I tried to get
through the checkout without a ticket to fly.

I visited mother, who gave me a tour of her vandalised house.
My resolve to fly away hardened. The phantom had put cheese
parings down the back of the Chesterfield, stolen the feathers
out of a favourite cushion and painted the paws in a print of

33

Renoir's *Girl with Cat* a darker shade of white.

I had a blouse for Rosie but no ship to carry it to her. She emailed her disappointment in Wragg and didn't know what he'd done to get into trouble with the French authorities. The only alternative boat from Mangareva was the *Braveheart*, chartered by the British government solely to carry judges, police officers and government officials to Pitcairn for the trials.

From his cellphone in Auckland its captain, Nigel Jolly, said I could sail with him at the beginning of August. He'd need clearance from the British authorities because he didn't want to jeopardise his contract with them, but there was no problem with the French – he was a friend of the customs officer in Mangareva. Vic Young, great-great-great-grandson of the mutineer Edward Young, who went to Pitcairn with Fletcher Christian, would be a passenger too. I rebooked flights with Harold Wing – a flexible return to Tahiti and a five-Polynesian-island pass. But Jolly was never there when I phoned and didn't respond to my messages. I decided to try to sail to Pitcairn from Auckland on a cargo ship, though this would mean bureaucratic scrutiny, a licence to land and the cost of again changing tickets.

Disclaimers and conditions on the Pitcairn Council application form for a licence seemed designed to discourage. Licences were rarely granted. Anyone who landed without one was liable to a fine of a thousand dollars. The Council accepted no responsibility for damage or loss of property, personal injury, accident or death during any visit or while landing or departing. Return travel arrangements were a matter of chance and visitors might be marooned for months while waiting for a ship. Charter yachts from French Polynesia were prohibitively expensive. There were no hotels, banking facilities or medical services on the island. Licensees must be of good behaviour and obey the island's laws.

I cited an interest in Pitcairn's flora and fauna as my reason for wanting to visit. Herb Ford of the Pitcairn Islands Study Center in Angwin, California, had advised me not to mention anything about writing books. 'I must warn you', he wrote, 'that if you brag in any way of your authorial feats you may be escorted summarily off the island.' I wondered how this could happen in the absence of a ship.

Shirley, the commissioner's personal assistant in the Pitcairn Office in Auckland, was discouraging about shipping from New Zealand. It had never been more difficult. The once trusted P&O liner no longer sailed. There was a cargo ship in September but no free berth on it: Pitcairners returning home and officials had priority. The company Seatrade New Zealand took all bookings and she never knew until three or four weeks before departure if there was any space. There might be two small cruise ships, *Amazing Grace* and *Clipper Odyssey*, calling at the island, but all was vague.

Verity said the journey wasn't meant to be and I should find a calmer approach to life. I thought that if Bligh had been calmer with Christian and made him feel valued, perhaps he wouldn't have found himself in an open boat at the edge of life and at the mercy of the violent ocean. He'd have taken the pot plants to the West Indies, then they'd all have gone home to Deptford.

Still I longed for a ship and the wide sea. I went on preparing as if a journey was assured. I bought a medical kit, water-purifying tablets, Deet and Imodium, a silk vest, a compass, a woollen hat and a dual-faced clock that told the time in two chosen parts of the world.

On a morning when I was thinking of something else an email came from the Pitcairn Office in Auckland. Shirley had news, she wrote, that would turn my day upside down. A supply ship, the *Tundra Princess,* was leaving the port of Tauranga in seven days. There was a berth on it. It was carrying a cargo of kiwi fruit to Amsterdam via Panama and it would make a brief stop at Pitcairn to unload supplies for the islanders. I should email my passport and credit card details if I wanted to go. I'd need warm clothes, wet-weather gear, stuff for seasickness and something to do on the journey. 'There's a lot of water to cross,' she wrote. She'd book a hotel for me in Auckland. I should get to Tauranga by 26 June, but the crew wouldn't load the kiwi fruit if it was raining. She again warned there was no assured passage off Pitcairn. On two occasions people marooned there had been so desperate to leave they'd paid Seatrade, at great cost, to divert a ship to pick them up.

I phoned mother and told her I was going on a journey. Good, she said, would I bring her back some smoked salmon. It was a long journey, I said, to the other side of the world, to a remote island in the middle of the Pacific and the nearest large land mass was New Zealand. Why did I want to do that? she asked. I said it was to do with my work. Her rejoinder was that I didn't know the meaning of work and how was she supposed to manage if I went off to New Zealand?

I said a good thing about her having several children was that we shared the load, the others would look after her while I was gone, but it was a worry to us all that she shooed away professional carers and lived alone under siege in a house she could no longer manage. She replied that no agent of the devil would drive her from her home. Did I remember her Georgian glass tankard, her Lalique vase, her Cobra green claret jug, art nouveau decanter, perfume bottles, case of stuffed birds, Millefiori paperweight, blue enamelled carriage clock, Chinese ivory snuff bottle, her Liberty sideboard? All were now chipped, smeared, marked and vandalised.

I tried colluding with her paranoia. When did this person call? I asked. She didn't know, she hadn't been out, the doors were locked, the windows too. I began to think that no island was remote enough for the journey I hoped to make, that my quest was for departure and not to reach a destination, that I could not leave the frozen heart of my relationship with Verity and that my mother's madness was a strait through which no ship could pass.

II

TAURANGA TO BOUNTY BAY

*Anywhere can be a destination. Usually we arrive
where we choose to go*

11

The Pitcairn Commissioner's office was on the tenth floor with views of Auckland's Bay of Plenty and wharves. Trevor Murray wore a blue shirt of wifely creaselessness. He'd just returned on a supply ship via Panama from two months on Pitcairn. On his new flat-screened computer were 351 unanswered email.

He didn't question why I wanted to visit the island and I again volunteered my interest in the flightless rail. He said I should remember I was going to an entirely isolated community. The impending trials had divided family against family and everyone on Pitcairn was, or was related to, a victim or defendant. Lawyers, judges and journalists were about to swarm there, ferried from Mangareva on the *Braveheart*. I thought of the newspaper reports of abusive sex with underage girls. I'd not dwelt on the details which seemed squalid.

Murray told me to buy wellington boots and take no valued clothes, because when it rained, red volcanic mud splashed everywhere. Pitcairners went barefoot but visitors needed shoes. I should observe the island's customs and go to church. Rosie and her husband were very devout. They preached the sermon in church for there was now no pastor on the island. They didn't drink alcohol, tea or coffee, or smoke or trade on the Sabbath and they said grace before all meals. It would be acceptable, though, if I bought a liquor licence and took wine with me to have with my food.

I thought of Rosie's blouse and feared I'd chosen unwisely. I wondered why I was going to a place inhabited by sex offenders where I'd not be wanted and I'd confound some notion of God if I had a drink. I said I liked swimming. Murray spoke of a natural pool formed by seawater at St Paul's Point – beautiful, but too cold in August, which was winter in these Pacific islands. Waves might break with great force over the rocks. Many of the place names of Pitcairn were in memory of accidents: Nellie Fall, Robert Fall, Dan Fall, McCoy's Drop. 'Have no illusion,' he said, 'you're going to a very primitive place.'

He talked of projects to improve shipping, extend the jetty, lay a concrete road, generate electricity by the wind, encourage ecological tourism and provide a boat for tourist trips to Henderson Island. I liked his practical cast of mind. He said theft was unknown on the island. There was barter, kindness and no hunger. Pitcairners liked fried food and a lot of it and there was a problem with obesity and diabetes. A locum from New Zealand was there for three months giving dietary advice, but Rosie's food was good and I'd eat avocados and mangoes, pawpaw, passion fruit, salads and fish.

Shirley, his personal assistant, sprucely dressed and with a no-nonsense air, checked my papers and payments. I signed a disclaimer for Seatrade in case anything disastrous happened to me on the *Tundra Princess*, an assurance that I was not carrying anything to do with bee-keeping, and I paid twenty-five dollars for my liquor licence. I was to carry flu vaccines, in an envelope padded with ice slabs, for two of the island's elderly, and a new watch for Rosie because hers had broken. I was to instruct the captain of the *Tundra Princess* to store these vaccines in the ship's fridge, and give him a letter thanking him for carrying me, one other passenger, the vaccines, mail, supplies and other items. These included gas cylinders, and the perimeter fence for the prison the island's men were themselves building and where they'd be incarcerated if found guilty of the offences for which they'd been charged.

Shirley warned me not to take sides over the islanders' claims and counterclaims concerning the trials. I should be non-committal, have no opinions and say only 'Oh really' or 'Oh yes'. She, too, warned against wearing anything but shorts and T-shirts because of the dreaded mud. It would never wash out – not from trainers, jeans, not from anything. I should forget about make-up and appearance. I'd get up in the morning, pull on yesterday's clothes and run my hands through my hair.

The *Tundra Princess* was to leave on 2 July. The dangerous part of the voyage was getting off the ship into the Pitcairn longboat down a rope ladder, two or three miles offshore from the island. In twelve years they'd not lost anyone, but there'd been near misses in bad weather. She warned yet again that leaving the island would be difficult and special arrangements costly. I should contact her by email two months before I wanted to leave, but she couldn't say how long it would then take to find a ship.

In Tauranga she'd reserved a room for me in the Pacific Motor Inn. She gave me the mobile number of the shipping agent who'd issue my embarkation instructions and take me through customs formalities. There would, she said with a grimace and a laugh, be another passenger on board. 'An admiral's wife. A most unusual woman. She'll be company for you. The crew's all men.'

In the lobby of the Domain Lodge in Auckland I downloaded email from my brothers about mother. She'd overdosed on diazepam and was in hospital. She was conscious, but thought my brother was the milkman. A neighbour, woken in the night by her smoke alarm, had broken a window, crawled through it and found her on the hall floor, a burnt-out milk saucepan on the lit gas ring and a scorch mark on the kitchen ceiling. Social Services said she'd be at risk if she returned to her house and a place was reserved for her at Sunset View. The fees were £600 a week and her house and possessions were to be sold to finance this. Was there anything I wanted before it all went to the auction rooms?

Beyond the hotel window I observed the high blue sky and unfamiliar vegetation: palm ferns and mango trees, bougain-villea and frangipani, hibiscus and bromeliads. I didn't want any of my mother's possessions. Possessions were a poor sub-stitute for something I'd wanted but failed to find.

12

The ordeal of the nineteen men forced into an open boat by Fletcher Christian lasted seven weeks, from 28 April until 14 June 1789. When they stopped at one of the Friendly Islands, the quartermaster John Norton was beaten to death with stones by tribesmen as he ran down the beach to cast off the stern of the boat. After that, unarmed, starving, dependent, bearing no gifts and like spectres of death, the surviving men didn't dare land on any inhabited island.

For sixteen days in continual rain they were squashed together, soaking wet and numb with cold, with swollen legs, violent gut pains, aching bones and little use of their limbs. They bailed night and day as great waves broke over the boat. Sleep 'in the midst of water' was no comfort. Dinner was a bit of coconut or a morsel of pork or bread. On a morning when to their great joy they hooked a fish, the creature writhed and returned to the sea. When the sun rose fiery and red, wind storms followed. If it shone at noon, they were scorched by its heat. There were nights so dark they couldn't see each other, days when they were equally blinded by rain and seawater. When the weather raged, they could do no more than run with the tide. The least error at the helm might in a second cause their destruction.

Even on this terrible voyage Bligh took confident, galling command, convinced of 'God's gracious support' and his own superiority. As ever he had a goal. He would get himself and these men to the Dutch colony of Timor. From there they could get passage to England. He calculated the voyage would take eight weeks, so he rationed such provisions as they had, to last for ten. He meted out equal starvation rations in scales made of coconut shells. Bullets – 'pistol balls' found by chance in the boat – were his weights. When they caught a booby bird he divided it into eighteen portions and gave its blood to the three men nearest death. With each measured portion of beak, entrails or claws he called, 'Who shall have this?' in a display of fairness. He called the torrential rain a blessing, for constant sun would have scorched them and killed them from thirst. He contrived a canvas weather cloth round the boat, threw inessential stuff overboard for balance and speed and supervised men to watch and bail. He made them all wring their clothes in seawater each morning because he thought this refreshing, and he stored the bread in the carpenter's tool chest.

He described the mutineers as 'a tribe of armed ruffians... unfeeling wretches'. He'd account to his king and country and bring them to the gallows:

A few hours before, my situation had been peculiarly flattering. I had a ship in the most perfect order and well stored with every necessary both for service and health: by early attention to particulars I had, as much as lay in my power, provided against any accident in case I could not get through Endeavour Straits, as well as what might befall me in them; add to this the plants had been successfully preserved in the most flourishing state, so that, upon the whole, the voyage was two-thirds completed, and the remaining part in a very promising way; every person on board being in perfect health, to establish which was ever among the principal objects of my attention.

In his journal he wrote that these ruffians turned against him because of the 'allurement of dissipation' on Tahiti, where sex was freely available and they need never work, where the chiefs protected them and gave them land, where the sun shone and the food was good. They were 'void of connections' in their own country whereas he, a family man, understood responsibility. They were scheming villains who'd deceived their trusting leader. 'The possibility of such a conspiracy was ever the farthest from my thoughts,' he wrote.

46

Anger and vengeance would get him the 3600 miles to Timor. His testimony would be believed. The mutineers had committed a great crime for which the ultimate punishment awaited them. He'd see Christian dead.

13

Sitting on a box by the quayside at Tauranga port on 2 July 2004 was a woman in her fifties with bright blonde hair and sunglasses on a beaded chain round her neck. She wore a padded gold jacket and white snow boots. I'd seen her before on the coach from Auckland to Tauranga. She was hard to overlook. As we drove past orange, lemon and olive groves and fields of sheep she'd sung in a clear soprano 'Soave sia il vento' from *Così Fan Tutte* and 'Evil Deeds' by Eminem. I supposed her to be accompanying what was on her iPod. At the comfort stop at Thames she ordered vegetable soup and a caramel milk shake then missed the coach. We waited for her two miles on, at the Rendezvous Motel.

'Thank you, drivah,' she said as she reboarded, without a hint of contrition for causing inconvenience. After ten minutes she called, 'Drivah, you're going too fast. And in England you'd be fined on the spot for using a mobile phone.' The driver, a young energetic-looking man, muttered in Maori. I and another woman exchanged a grimace.

In Tauranga from high on Mount Maungani I'd watched the *Tundra Princess* towed by pilot boats into the harbour, a white, silent ship on blue water. Walking the path at the foot of the mountain, where yellow-beaked birds nested in pohutukawa trees, I heard again that penetrating voice. 'You don't get many shags in Knightsbridge.' She was addressing a passer-by. Later in the day, walking round residential streets, I saw her feeding grain into the mailboxes by the garden gates.

It didn't occur to me she'd be travelling to Pitcairn. In his office, the shipping agent, Keith Thompson, had told me about the voyage. He had bright eyes and a ginger moustache and didn't himself travel by sea because he was always sick. He said the *Tundra Princess* had an all-Indian crew of twenty-two men. Seatrade used Indian or Filipino labour because it was cheapest. He hoped I liked curry. If I wanted less spicy food I should buy it before I boarded. The other passenger, Lady Myre, was taking a large quantity of pot noodles with her.

He told me the ship's cargo of kiwi fruit, bound for Europe, had been picked in May and was packed in containers kept at 0.8 degrees and checked by a full-time refrigeration engineer. It would take at least seven days and nights for the ship to reach Pitcairn and about seven hours to unload the islanders' supplies into their longboats. In heavy seas the captain wouldn't stop. He'd go on to Panama then Zeebrugge. There was a third woman on board besides Lady Myre and me, an officer's wife. Probably I'd have my own cabin, but it was up to the captain.

I supposed that the bedizened figure alone on the quayside was Lady Myre. I was curious why she was there, and about the incident of the grain in the mailboxes. As if she'd read my thoughts, or perhaps because of the terns that swooped overhead and dived low in curiosity, she told me she loved birds and how sweet the New Zealanders were to put little houses

48

for them at the entrance to their gardens. I didn't tell her she'd been filling their mailboxes with seed. Her eyes were translucent blue. 'Lady Maar,' she said with no apparent appraisal of me. 'Pot noodles,' she said, indicating the box on which she sat. 'Enough for a fortnight. Just add boiling water.' She asked me if I'd been to India. I said I hadn't. 'You should,' she told me. 'It's *wunderbar,* but all they eat is curry. Makes your eyes water and gives you the runs.'

I sat with her on her noodles. 'It's a heck of a large ship for Picton,' she said. 'I was only expecting a ferry.' I agreed it was indeed a large ship – of 17,000 tons – and, as I understood it, Picton was on New Zealand's South Island, but the *Tundra Princess* was bound for Zeebrugge, with a change of crew at Panama, and it was only calling at Pitcairn for the islanders to come out in their boats to collect their supplies. I didn't doubt others must have given her the same information. She seemed incurious about facts. She said she supposed none of it mattered and that she and Garth would meet up if this was meant to be.

There followed a confusing story about Garth Dutton, a half-brother, who a decade previously had gone to New Zealand to escape an unsatisfactory marriage and a failed business. She'd tried to trace him through the internet, but now destiny would intervene. She asked me my star sign and told me she was Pisces and drawn to all things watery.

I feared she'd be an exigent co-passenger. She said her husband Sir Roland, a retired admiral, would always get her out of any fix. They'd first met in New York on Riis Beach in bay

49

six. She'd known he was her man when he'd rescued her swimming hat from a frenzied Pekinese. '*Très galant,*' she said. 'Quite fearless.' They'd been married twenty-seven years and shared a love of the sea. When single she'd worked on a cruise ship, the *Southern Star,* as entertainment staff. She was vague as to where she'd cruised. 'Round the world,' she said, with a wide, circling motion. 'Round and round.' They did six shows over and over and her special numbers were 'Somewhere over the Rainbow' and 'Blow the Wind Southerly'. 'Encores galore.'

She asked if I'd acquired a liquor licence and I pointed to my carton of wine and two litres of Glenfiddich. She'd been accorded the owner's cabin, and her crate of rum and cans of peach juice were already in it with the rest of her luggage. 'I could do with a snort now,' she said.

I had no sense of common ground. I told her how Bligh, in his open-boat navigation to Timor, rationed the men to a teaspoon of rum at daybreak when their limbs were numb with cold. I said how uncertain shipping was off Pitcairn and how the desperate paid four thousand dollars to divert a ship to collect them. 'I know all that,' she said. 'I'm not bothered. If there are any problems, Roley will sort them.'

She asked why I was travelling to Picton. I warmed again to my interest in chaos theory and the mutiny on the *Bounty* – how the theft of a coconut by Fletcher Christian and the intense relationship between him and William Bligh had as one of its tangential ramifications the fact that I was now to sail on the *Tundra Princess* to Pitcairn Island with her. I spoke of how tectonic plates move beneath the earth's surface and in time spew up islands that become worlds in microcosm, how islands sink and coral grows and atolls form, and reefs.

Her glazed look made me suppose she was as uncertain of me as a travelling companion as I of her. She asked what tectonic meant and I said in a knowing way that it was a Greek word meaning carpenter and that geologically it referred to processes that affect the earth's crust. She said I was cute and reminded her of a marmoset. She told me how she'd stayed as a guest on Marlon Brando's island of Tetiaroa, how pathetically inappropriate his accent had been when he played Fletcher Christian, how he'd weighed over twenty stone when he died in an oxygen tent at the age of eighty, how Jack Nicholson then bought his house in Beverly Hills for five and a half million dollars and that it wasn't true that Brando got through all those millions of royalties, he'd stashed it all away – that was what men did – and if she ever divorced Roley, which she wouldn't because he was such a dear even though he did have a roving eye and a liking for a tot or two, she'd make quite sure she got the Manor House at Little Nevish because to lose that would be like losing her right arm, her *soul*, she said, and fear suffused her translucent eyes. Nor could she lose her Knightsbridge flat. She had her personal dresser in Harrods – Martina – who filled a rail with possibles every month. But, like most men, Roley had to have control of the money. It was power.

I hoped that in making the same journey as I, Lady Myre would not invade the solitary, dreamy lonely place in my mind. I feared that like my mother and Verity, she threatened to oust my new-found interest in eighteenth-century mariners who traversed the world when it was an unknown globe of wonders and adventures.

14

Bligh wrote in his log that the mutineers called 'Huzzah for Tahiti' as they jeered at his plight and turned from their crime. That they sailed in the wrong direction – west-north-west – he took as a feint to deceive him. But Christian knew he'd find no safety on Tahiti. A ship would seek him and take him in irons to England to a sensational trial and a public hanging with his family vilified. And the Tahitians would view with suspicion his return without Bligh. Suspicion led to retribution. He knew how ominous Polynesian hostility could be: the clapping of conch shells, the grouping of pirogues, the slinging of stones with the force of cannon, the hacking to pieces of a man deemed an enemy. There was fear in the Polynesian soul of these light-skinned, brazen strangers who killed with gunfire while hidden from sight. Staying alive was more important to Christian than meeting again with one or several Tahitian women whose names he'd not learned to say.

He took command of the *Bounty*. He was its captain now. He occupied Bligh's cabin and wore Bligh's clothes: his dimity waistcoats, silk stockings and shirts, silver buckles and nankeen breeches. He took Bligh's sword, pistols and fowling piece. Crucially, he appropriated his charts, maps, notes and books. Among these were James Cook's *Voyage to the Pacific Ocean*, John Hawkesworth's *Account of Discoveries in the Southern Hemisphere*, William Dampier's *Discourse of Voyages* and

Discourse on Winds, both George Anson's and Louis Bougainville's *Voyage Round the World* and Alexander Dalrymple's *Voyages and Discoveries in the Pacific Ocean.*

These works had informed Bligh's skill as a navigator. With them Christian had enough reference to find his way to wherever he chose to go. He also had plans of harbours, two sextants, a spyglass, three compasses and books on *The Scurvy, The Health of Seamen, Hot Climates,* on Euclid, chemistry, and electricity. He had David Hume's *History of England* and the *Bounty*'s Bible and Prayer Book.

The *Bounty* was on no commercial venture now. Christian ordered that any two men in conversation be joined by a third. He pocketed the keys to the liquor store to avoid drunkenness and to safeguard the supply of port, brandy and three hundred gallons of Tenerife wine. And with hatred for Bligh he had the entire cargo of breadfruit plants thrown into the sea.

Christian's survival now depended on lies and cunning. He'd taken a coconut to quench his thirst and consequences followed. He needed a place to hide. He chose the island of Tubuai as his destination. His plan was to go there to reconnoitre and map out an area of settlement, then return to Tahiti with some contrived explanation, abduct women and builders, and collect essential supplies.

Charted by Cook, Tubuai was 398 miles south of Tahiti and circled by a barrier reef with only a single pass through it. Christian sighted it on the afternoon of 28 May 1789, a month after the mutiny. He sent an armed cutter, with the midshipman George Stewart in charge, to explore the opening through the reef. Stewart was a small-faced, dark-eyed, skinny man, with a heart and arrows tattooed on his left arm. Tubua-ians in their canoes approached to guide him. That done, they pilfered what they could from his boat. Stewart terrified them with gunfire and they sped to the shore and the cover of trees.

Next day the *Bounty* passed through the gap in the reef and anchored in the lagoon. Christian observed the stretch of the island, the wide lagoon, the fringe of silver sands and coconut palms. Here was a lush place of fertile valleys, concealing mountains, streams and waterfalls, another Paradise of the World.

Tubuaian tribesmen grouped on the sand armed with stones, spears and lances. They blew into conch shells and approached the *Bounty* in canoes. A chief, an old man, ven-tured on board and marvelled at the ship. Christian gave him nails and red feathers. The chief seemed honoured but was afraid of the creatures he'd never seen before – pigs, dogs and goats, the stench of them and the despairing noise they made.

In another canoe young women garlanded with flowers sang, clapped, moved in rhythm and enticed the sailors who responded with beads and propositions. Fifty more canoes quickly circled the ship. The men in them blew conch shells, beat drums, clambered on to the ship and took what they could. One grabbed the ship's buoy, another the main com-pass. Christian snatched the compass back and lashed at the man with a rope. The islanders leapt into the water or back into their canoes. They made a terrific noise, waved lances, showered the ship with spears and stones and drove their canoes at it. The mutineers responded with fire from pistols and muskets. Within minutes a dozen Tubuaians, among them a garlanded woman, lay dead or dying in the bay.

Christian then rowed to the shore. He explored the concealing mountains, the lush wooded valleys, the protection of the reef, the rich larder of fish and fruit. He tried to offer the islanders reparative gifts of axes, goats and pigs, but they ran away when he approached. Undeterred, he kept to his plan to return to Tahiti to procure provisions and women, then come to this perfect place to build a fortress as a settlement. The Tubuaians renamed the bay where he'd arrived the Bay of Blood.

15

I had a cabin to myself, the 'master's cabin', adjacent to Captain Dutt's. Pandal the steward showed me to it. He rightly thought it grand, with its private bathroom, wardrobe, seascapes on the walls, sofa, reading lamps, fridge filled with bottled water, juices and cola. In an opposite room was a Zanussi washing machine and tumble-dryer. Pandal smiled with pride and kept asking, 'Good?' I didn't know a word of Hindi. 'Good,' I repeated. 'Good. Very good.'

Captain Dutt was plump, with small hands and feet and delicate gestures. He wore a baseball cap and when he was worried the skin on his scalp wriggled, which made the cap move backwards and forwards. He was thirty-eight but looked older. He pined to be home in Mumbai with his wife and eight-year-old daughter. He'd joined the *Tundra Princess* seven months previously in Cape Town and was scheduled to fly home from Panama.

He was agitated by the arrival of Lady Myre and me, the flu vaccine that had to be refrigerated, the prospect of delays and complications because of the Pitcairn stop. He wanted a swift, trouble-free journey, but his deep courtesy prevailed.

Melancholy was behind all he said, a disappointment with his fate. He was tired of the constraints and demands of life at sea. He spoke of missed opportunities and the regrets these provoked. 'We have to seize our chances,' he said. 'Our opportunities are few.' His head jiggled with memories. He'd earned the rank of captain when he was twenty-nine. Three years ago his employers had promised him a shore job, but it hadn't materialised and now he'd heard it wouldn't. He was a good captain, so it was in their interest to keep him in charge of a ship. He needed more crew but was allowed only the minimum. The workload was tiring for a complement of twenty-two men and they had little rest. And this ship had a broken bilge keel, bent on one side, missing on the other, which made it roll to starboard if the weather was bad. Extra vigilance was required to keep the kiwi fruit from damage. A repair would mean putting the ship in dry dock at great expense. He'd make two more voyages for this company then leave. He'd take a year's course in Cardiff then work in marine insurance.

He told me I might send and receive email from his computer via the ship's satellite. If I wrote out what I wanted to send, he'd sort it for me. I was free to go to the bridge to look at the navigation charts and radar screens. I'd eat with him and his officers in their mess room. If I didn't like Indian food

56

his cook, who was from Goa and very good, was happy to serve continental food too.

From the quarterdeck I watched two pilot boats tow the *Tundra Princess* from the quayside at Tauranga to the deep water of the Pacific. It was a cold late-afternoon. A mile out, the clutter of the harbour receded and the wind and swell picked up. The pilots waved as they cast off the ropes and turned their boats to the shore. The sea looked dark blue and a reflection shimmered over it of the setting sun. Captain Dutt told me the horizon was sixteen miles away and that was the limit of our vision.

Nothing was familiar except the excitement and melancholy of departure. I thought how some people have difficulty reconciling their inner self with the outer world, and perhaps I was such a person. I wondered why I didn't live by an abiding connection to someone or some place when I so yearned for home. I drafted an email for Verity and my brothers: 'I am safely at sea. My quarters are very comfortable. You can email me if you want.'

Supper in the officers' mess began at six. There was chicken curry, daal and vegetables. Men drifted in, ate what they wanted, then left. Da Silva, the chief engineer, welcomed me. He was from Goa and a Catholic. He told me that most of the crew were Hindus and that there were no Muslims on board. He had sleek black hair and knife-edge creases in his trousers. He crossed himself before he ate and said he had to have meat or fish with every meal. His cousin had recently been killed in a motorbike accident, so he wore a black sleeve band of mourning. His wife and daughter were in hospital when this happened. His daughter had dysentery after eating potato balls bought from a roadside stall, and a bolt had lodged in his wife's head when her pressure cooker exploded. She had to have thirty stitches.

Lady Myre didn't listen to these familial troubles. She wore a luminous yellow lifejacket over a puce T-shirt and avidly ate her pot noodles. She kept summoning Pandal for chapatti and fruit and she talked to the second engineer, Harminder Pal-singh, who was from the Punjab, about her time in Calcutta with the viceroy and her punkah wallah.

There was a mood of order and reserve among the company in which I found myself. Harminder piled his plate with food and had a kirby grip in his beard. Both Da Silva and the first officer, Jaswinder Singh, were silent when he talked and didn't look at him. Jaswinder's wife Soni was the third woman on board. They'd been married two years and for the first year he'd been away at sea. This time she was sailing with him. She'd put on a stone in weight after seven months on the ship, with three meals a day and no exercise. She'd never been separated from her parents before and was terribly homesick. At home she had a guru who taught her how to pray, and she missed his guidance. Each day she offered different prayers for the ruling god of the day: Krishna, Kali, Shiva, Shakti, Indra, Brahma and Ganesh, the one that looked like an elephant. Her life, she said, was in service to her gods, her guru and her husband. Above all things she wanted to please them.

Three days a week she ate only vegetarian food in deference

to the gods that appreciated this. She offered to show me the devotional paintings she'd done on this voyage. She seemed happy with her husband and respectful of him, though he shared none of her religious interests. The polite reserve between them was like liberation from the test of intimacy.

Captain Dutt sat at the head of the table and seemed absorbed in his own thoughts. He ate only orange segments, so I wondered why he was overweight. He explained that on Wednesday 7 July the ship would cross the International Date Line, which meant we'd have two Wednesdays. This news discombobulated Soni, who would like to have consulted her guru as to whether she should eat only vegetables two days running in deference to Wednesday's god.

After supper Lady Myre went to the officers' mess to watch a video of *Ben Hur*. She asked me to join her, but I said I was going to my cabin to work. What work was that? she asked, and the question discomfited me. Two A4 sheets of email, marked for my attention, had been slipped under the door. One was from my brother. Mother was now in Sunset View on the Aurora floor. Her room was pleasant, though small, and the staff were sensible, but her delusional state had worsened. She wouldn't take her medication or eat any food because she thought she was being poisoned. She'd thrown her washing things out of the window then accused the staff of stealing them. They felt they couldn't cope with her. She kept phoning 999 to say she'd been beaten up. With guilt I felt it ought be in my power to put things right, though I knew that wasn't true.

Verity emailed that she was pleased I was safe at sea. She was taking a research job in Wivenhoe and would move there within a month. Our stuff would be stored and she was glad I had Mill Cottage to go to in the interim.

Work seemed a refuge. I made a chronological list of important dates:

1754 9 September. William Bligh born in Plymouth.
1764 25 September. Fletcher Christian born in Cumbria.
1767 2 July. Captain Philip Carteret, in HMS *Swallow* discovers Pitcairn Island.
1779 14 February. Bligh sees Captain Cook hacked to pieces by islanders in Kealakekua Bay, Hawaii.
1780 May. Fletcher Christian's mother declared bankrupt. She moves her family to Douglas on the Isle of Man.
      June. Bligh returns home to Douglas after the fateful journey with Cook.
1781 4 February. Bligh marries Betsy Betham.
1785 July. Christian writes to Bligh and asks for a place as midshipman.
1786–7 Bligh and Christian voyage together.
1787 23 December. The *Bounty* sails from Spithead for Tahiti.
1788 2 March. Bligh makes Christian his acting lieutenant and executive officer.
      28 March. Terrible storms at Cape Horn.
      22 April. Bligh gives up trying to round the Horn. He turns the *Bounty* and heads for Tahiti via Africa and the Cape of Good Hope.
      26 October. The *Bounty* arrives at Matavai Bay, Tahiti.
      November. Breadfruit potting begins.
      9 December. Dr Huggan the surgeon dies of alcohol poisoning.
1789 January. The *Bounty* nearly wrecked as it runs aground when shifting harbour in Tahiti. Anchor cable cut, probably by a Tahitian.
      5 January. Charles Churchill, William Muspratt and John Millward desert, but are recaptured.

February. Stored sails are found to be rotten. Discipline erodes. Resentment at Bligh's contempt and floggings.

4 April. The *Bounty* sails from Tahiti for the West Indies.

22 April. The *Bounty* anchors at Nomuka Island for supplies. The islanders are hostile to Christian and steal the anchor of his boat.

27 April. Coconut Day. Christian makes raft. Plans to jump ship.

28 April. Mutiny. Bligh and eighteen others set adrift in an open boat.

I doodled little boxes on my chronology. In my smart cabin I couldn't see the ocean, though I heard the boom from the engine room and felt the ship juddering against the waves. I pondered that it was a misapprehension to think the past could be discarded. Christian consigned his captain to the ocean, murdered Tubuaians, then supposed he could move away and start again. But he took mutiny and murder with him. He was not in a state of grace, though he might have hoped to find his new world pure.

And I... Historically daughters cared for their deranged ancient mothers. And it wasn't unreasonable of Verity to want a settled relationship, a partner to depend on and to wake up beside.

Wanting company, I braved *Ben Hur* and Lady Myre. She was sprawled alone on a leather sofa, had turned down the video's sound and was listening to her iPod. 'Don't you love Charlton Heston's legs?' she shouted. 'I'd die for legs like his.' I tried to watch soundless images of chariots and men in togas, but they enhanced my sense of confusion. 'The only line I like is "Your whole life is a miracle",' Lady Myre yelled. 'It makes me cry. I don't listen to the rest of it.'

Up on the bridge Captain Dutt worried about the weather. He'd received a shipping-forecast fax that warned of imminent gales and violent turbulence. He took off his baseball cap and his hair jiggled. He showed me the storm on the radar: swirling flecks of yellow, like in a kaleidoscope. We were heading into it. To avoid it, he'd have to alter course and go north then east, which would add two days to the journey to Pitcairn. He spoke again, and with anxiety, of eight thousand tonnes of kiwi fruit with a value of ten million dollars. He told me to hold on to the banister, go back to my cabin and be careful not to fall.

The *Tundra Princess* began to roll mightily. I banged against cabin furniture but knew that even with a damaged bilge keel this ship was untroubled by a force eight gale. I lay on my bed for safety and thought of the *Bounty* on its seemingly mundane breadfruit mission to Tahiti. The storms at Cape Horn... storms of wind, hail, sleet and tremendous waves, where the crew kept a fire alive day and night to dry their clothes, and the ship 'began to complain' and needed pumping every hour, and the decks were so leaky that hammocks had to be dried in the great cabin where all the plant pots were. I thought of the crew's relief when, after struggling for thirty days in this tempestuous ocean, Bligh turned the ship and headed east for the Cape of Good Hope. Bligh had no radar, email or satellite phone – no communication with anyone except a prayer to a god who was not often there...

Raja Arjunan, the second officer, knocked on my door with a

lifejacket and a safety familiarisation card. The radar screen showed we were in the middle of the storm, but nothing bad would happen, Raja said, because the gods were caring for this ship. But if there was an emergency I should muster on the boat deck by lifeboat number one. I'd be given a thermal suit and high-protein biscuits. The worst weather experience he'd known had been on a voyage from India to New York transporting marble for the twin towers memorial. A forecast from America warned of a hurricane. They'd gone north to avoid it but it changed direction and they steered into its eye.

He talked of the qualities that make a good captain. Because of the close proximity of shipboard life, the interdependent community and the perilous dangers, the captain, Raja said, must above everything be a manager of men. Politeness mattered, and encouragement. I thought of the words of Fletcher Christian's brother Charles, how 'jarring Discordancy' and 'repeated Acts of Irritation and Offence' were enough 'to change the Disposition of a Lamb into That of an Animal Fierce and Resentful'. Raja told me what a good captain Sanjeet Dutt was and how readily the men went to him with any problem. He listened, was fatherly, humorous and fair. He let them make decisions and have their freedom. They could send and receive email and use the satellite phone. He held lots of parties on board with barbecued food, dancing and fair shares of Hindi, Goan, Punjabi and Western music. On a voyage when the cook was hopeless he gave him a lot of time off, then helped the crew prepare their own food. He was decisive without being arrogant and had no air of superiority, rather he behaved as a humble man and did not flaunt his rank.

16

Bligh omitted from his journal incidents that didn't show himself as efficient and considerate, but his sailing master, John Fryer, claimed he was as tyrannical in the open boat as on the *Bounty*, that his chief concern was his own survival and, despite all the weighing with pistol shot and 'Who shall have this?' palaver, he took more bread for himself.

Bligh had an impenetrable self-regard and his underlying contempt and aggression made men hate him. He believed, rightly, that he showed his mettle in adversity. He achieved the extraordinary feat of reaching Timor with all the crew alive, in an ill-equipped boat, overloaded with men, on a journey without maps across violent seas. 'Wonderful as it may appear,' he wrote in his log, 'I felt neither extreme hunger nor thirst. My allowance contented me knowing I could have no more.' He broke his bread into slivers, dipped each bit in salt water and chewed it umpteen times to make it last longer.

He reached the coast of Australia after four horrendous weeks on 28 May 1789 – the same day as Christian in the *Bounty* reached Tubuai. The boat almost capsized as the men searched in high winds for an opening through the Great Barrier Reef. David Nelson the botanist was so weak he couldn't move. He had 'violent heat' in his bowels and he couldn't see. Bligh fed him morsels of bread soaked in wine. Within the calm of the reef they chanced on an uninhabited islet some two miles wide. As they pulled the boat ashore, one of the gudgeons broke from the rudder:

This if it had happened at sea would probably have been the cause of our perishing as the management of the boat could not have been so nicely preserved as these very heavy seas required. I had often expressed my fears of this accident and that we might be prepared for it had taken the precaution to have grummets fixed on each quarter of the boat for oars; but even our utmost readiness in using them, I fear would not have saved us. It appears therefore a providential circumstance that it happened at this place, and was in our power to remedy the defect; for by great good luck we found a large staple in the boat that answered the purpose.

The men made a fire by using a magnifying glass. They ate oysters and, against Bligh's advice, unknown berries. They'd observed birds eating them and though they feared the effects no one died. They saw bees, wasps, lizards and the tracks of a kangaroo. Bligh named the place Restoration Island, because with food, warmth and sleep the men were restored, and it was also the anniversary of the Restoration to the English throne of King Charles the Second.

Timor was still 1300 miles away and in a further ghastly week at sea, hatred of Bligh grew. There were two flare-ups when they stopped at another tiny rocky outcrop which he named Sunday Island. The men all gathered clams from the rocks, but William Purcell refused to hand his haul over. He said they were his. Bligh insisted they were common property and called him a scoundrel. Purcell said, 'If it wasn't for you, we wouldn't be in this mess.' Bligh grabbed a cutlass, threatened murder, and claimed the crew would all have perished without his command. Fryer intervened, wrestled with him and got the cutlass from him.

In another fracas, several men at midnight tried to snare

roosting birds barehanded, but caught only a dozen noddies. They blamed Robert Lamb, who'd separated from them and spoiled their chances by catching birds for himself. He confessed to being so desperate with hunger he'd eaten nine raw birds before rejoining the group. Bligh wrote in his journal that he gave him 'a good beating'. On previous days he'd written of how the men were more dead than alive, their clothes in rags, their extreme hunger evident, their appearance horrible, how they were skin and bone and covered in sores. Yet still he'd beat them.

After two more hellish weeks of starvation, sleeplessness and extremes of hunger, thirst, heat and cold, on Monday 15 June they reached the Dutch East Indian settlement of Coupang on the south-west shore of Timor. Bligh hoisted a makeshift flag of distress. The governor, William Adrian Van Este, received them with all kindness, a surgeon tended them and they were given a house, bedding, food and clothes.

David Nelson the gardener died on 20 July – of 'Inflammatory Fever', Bligh said. At the start of the voyage Joseph Banks had told Nelson, 'The whole success of the undertaking depends ultimately upon your diligence and care.' Nelson, a quiet man, had with diligence and care cultivated, nurtured, tended and potted the breadfruit plants that Christian flung into the sea. He was buried behind the chapel at Coupang without a tombstone.

Bligh didn't help his crew sort their final passage home. At Coupang he was the only one who could access money through an agent. He bought a thirty-four-foot schooner for a thousand Rix dollars, named it HMS *Resource*, and in it took them to Batavia* escorted by two armed Indonesian schooners. They arrived on 1 October 1789. He then left for home on the first available ship, a Dutch vessel, the *Vlydte*, which sailed to South Africa on the sixteenth. He took only his clerk John Samuel, and his servant John Smith. John Fryer called him fraudulent, violent, self-interested and unconcerned in any caring way for the men he commanded.

Most of these men were very ill. Three died in Batavia: Thomas Hall seaman, Peter Linkletter the quartermaster and William Elphinstone master's mate. Robert Lamb died trying to get home and the acting surgeon Thomas Ledward wasn't heard of again. A surviving letter from him to his family spoke of Bligh's harshness.

The captain denied me, as well as the rest of the gentlemen who had not agents, any money unless I would give him my power of attorney and also my will, in which I was to bequeath to him all my property. This he called security. In case of my death I hope this matter will be clearly pointed out to my relations.

Thirteen of the nineteen men set adrift by Christian reached home. Bligh was the first to arrive. He landed at Portsmouth on 2 January 1790.

* In 1949 this was renamed Jakarta.

17

The *Bounty* had left Tahiti on 4 April 1789. Christian arrived back there on 6 June without his captain and most of the crew or any of the breadfruit plants. He'd rehearsed a lie for the Tahitians about what had happened. He said that when they stopped at the nearby island of Aitutaki for water, they met up with Captain Cook. Bligh and Cook were thrilled to be reunited and were going to form a settlement there. Bligh had dropped the idea of taking all those breadfruit to King George. Supplies were needed for this new enterprise, which Christian had been delegated to go back to Tahiti to acquire.

The Tahitians regarded Cook as their friend and teacher. Bligh hadn't told them about his murder at Kealakekua in February 1779. He'd been Cook's midshipman on the *Discovery*. As at Nomuka, the Kealakekua tribesmen had stolen the ship's cutter. In revenge, Cook tried to take their king hostage and carnage followed. For the Hawaiians their king was their soul. 'An immense Mob compos'd of at least 2 or 3 thousand People' retaliated. Cook's men fired at them. Cook was attacked, hit with a club, held under water, beaten with stones, then hacked to pieces. Bligh rushed to the English camp and shouted at them to 'strike the Observatorys as quick as possible'. Before he spoke, the men could see in his eyes 'the Shocking news that Captn Cook was kill'd'.

Christian and the others who returned to Tahiti had cut spare sails into nautical jackets in an effort to look like a uniformed crew. If the Tahitians had doubts about his story they didn't convey them. In exchange for the red feathers they thought sacred, and for nails, they gave Christian 460 pigs, most of them sows, fifty goats, numerous hens, cockerels, dogs and cats, and the bull and the cow that Cook had given to Chief Otoo on his third visit to the island in August 1777.

Christian enticed on board six Tahitian men and eighteen girls and women. To join a colonising enterprise with Captains Cook and Bligh on a nearby island sounded attractive. If it didn't work out they could be home in a week in a double-hulled canoe. None of these abducted passengers knew they'd be exposed to danger, hardship and extravagant abuse.

18

For four days on the *Tundra Princess* bad weather precluded parties or much progress through the sea. Cooking pots flew across the galley, chairs slid across the mess room and Pandal couldn't lay the table. Low pressure pursued the ship and there was a constant PAN PAN warning. In the vast, empty Pacific the swell of the waves set in, created momentum and was more of a problem than the wind.

Captain Dutt couldn't work at the desk in his cabin because of the roll of the ship. He sat on the floor with a laptop, maps and faxes spread around him, playing Hindi music loud. Like a mantra he repeated that if the sea continued to be as wild as this he'd go straight to Panama. He was unfamiliar with Pitcairn's coast and dangers and had been told by his bosses not to anchor there.

In those stormy days I languished in my cabin or staggered to the galley for cups of sweet tea. Lady Myre flourished. She abandoned her pot noodles as bland, decided curry was a cure for queasiness, and ate her way through spicy mackerel, kedgeree and chicken vindaloo. Chilli made her eyes water and her cheeks flush. Around the ship she sang along with a medley of songs on her iPod: 'High on a Hill Lived a Lonely Goatherd' and 'Daddy Wouldn't Buy Me a Bow Wow'. The crew loved her and treated her like a trophy. She spent long hours in the officers' lounge watching videos: *Primal Fear, The Ghost Ship*, and *Death Wish* 1,2,3 and 4. She remained intractably on Greenwich Mean Time and carped at dinner being served in the middle of the night. I'd hear her imperious voice calling, 'Raja, you haven't replaced the towels in my cabin.' Raja would explain that he was the second officer, that towels were her responsibility, and that this was a cargo not a cruise ship.

Uninvited, she'd drift into my cabin and lie on my bed with her rum-and-peach-juice. She asked what I was scribbling. I told her I was making notes on the metaphor of the journey and the interconnection of voyages. She said if I wanted to know about voyages, I should look at the photos of her whitewater rafting in Ecuador and kayaking in Costa Rica. She'd been three inches away from a crocodile's jaws and found a scorpion under her pillow. She travelled with a company called Explore.

Twice she voiced surprise at the time the journey was taking. On the map, she said, Picton seemed close to Christchurch. I gave up trying to disabuse her about her destination. But I forcefully reiterated that Pitcairn was a rough place, the hideaway of the *Bounty* mutineers, that the population num-

bered only forty-nine, that many of the men were sex offenders and that nothing there would be easy. She laughed, said
God had a purpose for her which she was yet to find, and
asked me if I shaved my legs or used a depilatory.

I just couldn't fathom her. Because she so frequently
swigged, I told her this might be an offence on Pitcairn,
though I doubted she'd be gaoled if the prison was full. She
scrabbled in her bag for her liquor licence, waved it at me and
said she'd passed her drinking test. I explained that Pitcairners were Seventh Day Adventists who believed in the second
coming of the Messiah. She said she found the idea sweet and
wondered if they'd view her as their saviour. Roley often told
her she was no ordinary mortal. I again told her it might be
months before a ship called that would take her off the island.
She said she didn't care if she stayed until kingdom come.

In all I said I tried to discourage her from disembarking
with me. I hoped she'd stay with the *Tundra Princess* until
Panama. I feared she'd be a distraction, though I was fast losing focus as to what this distraction was from. I advised her
she could fly from Panama to Christchurch, then get a ferry to
Picton. She said she couldn't countenance an extra twenty-one
days on the ship alone with so many sailors. Her presence
would inflame them.

19

The *Bounty* with forty people on board reached Tubuai again
on 23 June 1789. This time Christian anchored on the western
side. Tribesmen paddled out to the ship without blowing

conch shells or waving lances. The chief of this area, Tummo-toa, went on board, accepted presents of red feathers, hatch-ets, nails and matting, pledged friendship to Christian and invited him to settle in his territory. He explained that the previous hostility came from a rival tribe governed by Chief Tinnarow.

Christian reconnoitred, looking for the best place for his proposed settlement. He favoured a site on the north-east coast, at Taahuaia, where there was a river, good vegetation, grazing land, a clear view of the lagoon and reef, and the chance to hide in the mountains. There was an abundance of breadfruit, coconuts, yams, bananas, fish and turtles. And the women, the sailors said, were the most beautiful they'd seen in the South Seas. This was where Christian hoped to build his new community, his colony, beyond the reach of English law.

The territory he chose was governed by a third chief, Taroatehoa. He, too, fêted Christian and, like Tummotoa, was pleased to receive red feathers and nails and keen for the mutineers to settle in his region. But Tummotoa viewed Christian's choice as an insulting rejection of his own hospi-tality. He told him and his crew never again to show them-selves in his or Tinnarow's territory. Two-thirds of the Tubu-aians now viewed these settlers as invaders. None the less Christian went ahead with plans for a wooden fort, fifty yards square, with a moat and a drawbridge facing the sea. It was to be guarded by swivel guns and cannons and called Fort George, in honour of the king whose laws he'd so flouted.

He instructed his crew and passengers to build this fort

during the day then return to the ship at sunset. But he couldn't enforce discipline. The mutineers, armed with pistols, drank, fought and threatened each other's lives. John Sumner and Matthew Quintal took to staying on shore at night to pursue women. On 5 July Christian had them put in leg irons. Two days later he and Charles Churchill drew up articles of agreement designed to impose rules and put aside past grievances. Each man was ordered to sign under oath. Sumner and Quintal signed, then said they were their own masters and would do as they pleased.

Not enough women had been taken from Tahiti for the men to have one each. The mutineers preyed on Tubuaian women. The midshipman George Stewart wrote that the men

began to Murmur and Insisted that Mr Christian would lead them, and bring Women in to live with them by force, and refused to do any more work till evry man had a wife, and as Mr Christian's desire was to perswade rather than force them, He positively refused to have any thing to do with such an absurd demand. Three days were Spent in debate and having nothing to employ themselves in, they demanded more Grog. This he also refused, when they broke the lock of the Spirit room and took it by force.

Mutiny, murder, abduction, rape and drunkenness were all on the agenda now. Scant progress was made in building Fort George. The Tubuaians grew to loathe this marauding gang who came, it seemed, from an uncivilised place. They suspected that the moat being dug was a communal grave intended for them. They ambushed a group of mutineers collecting coconuts and dragged Alexander Smith from the woman he was raping in the grass and took him, wearing only his shirt, to Chief Tinnarow's house. Christian's gang shot their way free, set fire to the house and stole emblems the Tubuaians regarded as gods.

Tinnarow wanted revenge for this arson, rape and pillage and for the slaughter of his people in the Bay of Blood. He plotted with one of the Tahitian men to murder the mutineers and seize the *Bounty*. News of this was conveyed to Christian by Mauatua, his Tahitian woman. In the fight that followed, sixty-six Tubuaians were killed, among them six women, Thomas Burkett was stabbed in the side by a Tubuaian spear and Christian wounded himself on his own bayonet. One of the Tahitians wanted to cut out the jawbones of the murdered men and hang them in the *Bounty* as trophies.

It occurred to most of the men on the *Bounty* that British justice might be no worse than the quality of freedom on offer. On 12 September, after less than three months and with not much constructed of Fort George, the ship left Tubuai for good. The intention was to return briefly to Tahiti. Those of the *Bounty* crew who chose to leave the ship there, could do so and await the consequences. The abducted Tahitian men and women were restrained and compelled to stay with Christian and the ship. His plan was to blow with the wind and colonise the first uninhabited island he chanced on.

The ship arrived back at Tahiti, at Matavai Bay, on the night of 22 September. It anchored a mile out to sea. Sixteen men were rowed ashore in the dark. Each was issued with a musket, pistol, cutlass, bayonet and ammunition. Eight mutineers opted to continue with Christian. The *Bounty* put out to sea while the women ate their supper. When they realised they'd been tricked, they were desperate. One woman leapt over-board about a mile outside the reef and swam for home on a moonless night. Next morning three other women were restrained from venturing to swim ashore as the ship passed the island of Tetiaro. Near Eimo, another of the Society Islands, two more women made such a fuss they were allowed to leave in a passing canoe. The rest sailed on: twelve Polyne-sian women and a baby girl, six Polynesian men and nine mutineers. They were to be the colonisers of Pitcairn Island.

20

In his journal Bligh wrote forensic descriptions of the wanted men, their scars, colouring and tattoos. Of the nine mutineers who sailed to Pitcairn he wrote:

FLETCHER CHRISTIAN master's mate aged 24 years, 5 feet 9 inches high, blackish or very dark complexion, dark brown hair, strong made; a star tatowed on his left breast, tatowed on his backside; his knees stand a little out, and he may be called rather bow-legged. He is subject to violent perspirations, and particularly in his hands, so that he soils any thing he handles.

EDWARD YOUNG midshipman aged 27 years, 5 feet 8 inches high, dark complexion and rather a bad look; dark brown hair, strong made, has lost several of his fore teeth and those that remain are all rotten; a small mole on the left side of his throat and on the right arm is tatowed a heart and dart through it with EY underneath and the date of the year 1788 or 1789.

JOHN MILLS gunner's mate aged 40 years, 5 feet 10 inches high, fair complexion, light brown hair, strong made and raw boned; a scar in his right arm pit occasioned by an abscess.

WILLIAM BROWN assistant botanist aged 27 years, 5 feet 8 inches high, fair complexion, dark brown hair, strong made; a remarkable scar on one of his cheeks which contracts the eye-lid and runs down to his throat, occasioned by the king's evil;* is tatowed.

JOHN WILLIAMS seaman aged 25 years, 5 feet 5 inches high, dark complexion, black hair, slender made; has a scar on the back part of his head, is tatowed and a native of Guernsey; speaks French.

ALEXANDER SMITH seaman aged 27 years, 5 feet 5 inches high, brown complexion, brown hair, strong made; very much pitted with the small pox and very much tatowed on his body, legs, arms and feet. He has a scar on his right foot, where it has been cut with a wood axe.

MATTHEW QUINTAL seaman aged 23 years, 5 feet 5 inches high, fair complexion, light brown hair, strong made; very much tatowed on the backside and several other places.

WILLIAM McCOY seaman aged 25 years, 5 feet 6 inches high, fair complexion, light brown hair, strong made; a scar where he has been stabbed in the belly, and a small scar under his chin; is tatowed in different parts of his body.

ISAAC MARTIN seaman aged 30 years, 5 feet 6 inches high, dark complexion, brown hair, slender made; a very strong black beard with scars under his chin, is tatowed in several places of his body.

Bligh delivered these descriptions of the Pitcairn settlers, as well as those of the men who returned to Tahiti, to the port authorities at Timor and Batavia. They were circulated to the Admiralty and to every ship that plied the South Seas.

* Scrofula: supposed to be cured by the touch of royalty.

21

On the fifth day on the *Tundra Princess* the wind abated and the sea calmed. Captain Dutt said if it was like this at Pitcairn, Lady Myre and I wouldn't have to climb down the Jacob's ladder to the longboats, he'd put the gangplank across.

He announced a party, to be held on the crew deck at seven. Frequent parties were part of his command. He held them when the ship crossed the equator or the International Date Line, if the weather was fine, if the crew had birthdays... I fretted about what to wear, for I'd brought only Rohan adventure clothes in my backpack. Pink sandals were my only concession to the party mood.

Lady Myre called for me. She shimmered like a tribal queen in purple silk and feathered hat, her lips crimson, her toenails green. She flashed a large sapphire ring. 'Don't you look cute,' she said. 'Just like a boy.'

We were guests of honour. The crew lined up to welcome us. They were not going to party until we arrived. Like a memsahib, Lady Myre dangled her fingers to the manner born. Some of the men bowed. Befuddled though she might be, she starred in the part. I was more of a problem in jeans, fleece and glasses, with incongruous pink sandals.

Speakers blared a mix of Indian and western music. There was a bar, a DJ, a barbecue. On a trestle table was a large bowl of vodka, tomato juice and Tabasco, glasses with frosted rims, plates of corn and spam fritters, and sandwich-spread on fried bread. Soni arrived late and looked exotic in a sari and flowing scarf but the crew took little notice of her because she was so wifely. They wore western clothes – jeans and sneakers, T-shirts with logos, or coloured shirts. Their dancing was energetic, sexy and unselfconscious. Sanjeet Dutt encouraged it for the same reasons as Bligh: as exercise, for conviviality and to reduce tension, but he was friendly and observant and took the measure of his men. I thought how when John Mills and William Brown refused to dance a jig at the obligatory hour Bligh stopped their supply of grog. It was not surprising they were among the mutineers.

Lady Myre knocked back Bloody Marys. She danced alone, waved her hands above her head and sang 'I Have a Dream' from her time on the Shaw Savill Line. She gave it all she'd got:

> Something good in everything I see.
> I believe in angels.
> When I know the time is right for me
> I'll cross the stream
> I have a dream.

The crew loved it and there was a cheer when she then asked Captain Dutt to dance. She took him by the hands and he beamed. Like a lot of fat men he was dainty on his feet.

She tried to get me to whirl about, but I wouldn't. After a ballroom number with Da Silva, she sat beside me and washed down spam fritters with another tumbler. In a slurry voice she asked Captain Dutt if there was much homosexuality on board. He said there was none. 'Believe that and you'll believe anything,' she hissed in my ear, then offered a complicated anecdote about when Sir Roland had picked up a marine in Skegness who'd pulled a gun on him and told him to keep driving. She then said I should keep my legs crossed, because a standing tool knows no conscience and a sailor from Goa wouldn't care about my age and strange appearance, for him a change would be as good as a holiday. Once again I advised her to stay on the ship until Panama.

Captain Dutt checked Raja from emptying another bottle of vodka into the Bloody Mary bowl. Harminder quaffed a tumbler of whisky. Prem, who was next on watch, drank only Coca-Cola. Pandal barbecued fish and vegetables. The wind made the coals flare, but Dutt saw the men could manage the incident and didn't intervene, though Lady Myre's ear was singed by a flying cinder of red-hot charcoal.

I didn't like not joining in and I wished I'd brought something snazzy to wear and could contribute and not be awkward. I thought how this was just one thing that was happening at a certain point in time: young Indian men dancing together in the middle of the Pacific Ocean on a cargo ship loaded with ten million dollars' worth of kiwi fruit, heading towards Pitcairn, the most isolated island in the world.

I left the party early, wanting to be alone.

The link between me and Verity weakened as the ship sailed on. In my cabin I mused on the past: the time we brought bay trees back on our bicycles from the flower market, the time we canoed on the River Brett and I steered us into the bank, the time we first kissed and she wondered about the origin of the cliché 'hook line and sinker', the times we tried to separate, but then went back. I wrote her an email, aware that Captain Dutt would read it and wonder about the passenger in the master's cabin.

Dear Verity

It's strange to receive email here in the middle of the Pacific Ocean with nothing in sight for days and nights but the sea. The journey's taking longer than expected because of pan pan weather, but hopefully we'll arrive at Pitcairn in two days' time. Life on board the *Tundra Princess* is very comfortable, the food's good, my cabin's luxurious and I eat with Captain Dutt and the officers in their mess room. There's one other passenger for Pitcairn, a strange woman called Lady Myre who seems to think she's travelling to Picton on New Zealand's South Island to be reunited with her long-lost half-brother. I think she's a bit soft in the head. Tonight there was a party on the crew deck, but I left early. I think of you and at times I wish you were making this journey with me.

Love etcetera

Lady Myre didn't show up for breakfast the morning after the party. I took coffee to her cabin. Her face looked unironed and grey roots sprouted from the blonde of her hair. She languished on her bed in a lemon silk housecoat, and she had a gold Alice band in her hair. She said her head ached because of there having been two Wednesdays and the clocks going forward an hour each day. All the cabin clocks were altered from the bridgehead in the night, which added to her confusion. She believed that the right time was that shown on her watch.

She seemed in a bad way. I told her it would be no big deal for her to fly home to London from Panama and that she was in no fit state to be buffeted by the waves in a longboat and then have to struggle up Pitcairn's Hill of Difficulty. She snivelled and said her whole life had been a hill of difficulty.

I told her she couldn't easily phone home from Pitcairn. She grizzled and said what did that matter – she'd no one to phone, no one loved her. She seemed unstable. But then her manner changed, she gave a sly look and said I was only goading her because I wickedly wanted to leave her alone with all these men. She patted the bedcover for me to sit beside her and said now she felt like girly talk. She closed her eyes and appeared to sleep. I sat on the fixed bench and talked winsomely of tectonic plates, island formations and the turbulence of tsunamis, but she didn't respond. She opened her eyes to slits, asked why I'd never been married and was there a significance to my wearing a ring on my little finger. 'Why should there be?' I replied. She seemed determined to be personal. She said she'd heard it was an indicator of homosexuality, but that wasn't always true. Roley's dear friend Colonel something-or-other was always lusting after some little darling and he wore a beautiful onyx on his pinky. Again I obfuscated. Though I'd no wish to conceal my sexual orientation, I feared frankness would disadvantage me on Pitcairn, given the teachings of Adventism. Nor did I want to disconcert the crew of the *Tundra Princess*.

I made some fatuous remark about how everything signified. She looked most comfortable reclining on her bed and I admired her unselfconscious ease. She said, 'It's clear you're not going to tell me anything about yourself. You're going to remain an enigma.' I didn't deny this. I asked if her husband minded her travelling alone and in such an unconventional way. 'Roley?' she said. 'No, he's such a dear. He doesn't mind what I do. He gave up trying to understand me the day after

81

we married. He knows that if I say I'm going to Singapore I'll end up in Saskatchewan and if I say I'll be away for a week it probably means a year.'

I pondered this information and how it fitted in with chaos theory and variations in patterns of random interconnected change. I supposed her provocative movements were because of her training as an actress and her year with the Shaw Savill Line. I asked if she felt like going up to the bridgehead to talk to Raja and Captain Dutt about our approach to Pitcairn. She said, much as she'd love to her head wouldn't allow it, so I went alone.

On the stairs I passed the cadet Salman Kanjee. He looked gaunt and hadn't slept. I'd thought him an arrogant young man but now he was deflated. He'd dropped all the keys to the stores out of the top pocket of his overalls into the sea. He'd checked that the containers of kiwi fruit were securely lashed, then bent over the side of the deck to look at the swirling waves. He feared he'd lose his job. The purser had received the news in silence. Some keys had no duplicates. It was a coveted position to be a cadet. Salman told me he was landsick – not homesick particularly, but sick of the sea. He wanted to walk down familiar streets, or sit in a café with a girlfriend.

On the bridgehead deck I looked out over the ocean and at the few intrepid seabirds that swirled in the ship's wake. Bligh had logged sight of porpoises, an albatross, blue petrels, shearwater, pintados, sharks, dolphins, whales and phosphorescent fish. Raja, who was keeping watch, said no creatures were visible in these deep cold waters. We might voyage for weeks and see no other sign of life, no other ship, no scrap of land.

He explained something of the wonder of the computer screens to me. To keep watch was essentially to observe a screen. Radar could pick up a ship twenty-four miles away. If something went wrong with the refrigerated containers – a loose connection or a swing in temperature – this would show up on the screen. But still the watchman at all hours surveyed the sea with his eyes and still in nil visibility he'd sound the ship's horn every minute.

Raja said people might think of life at sea as exotic, but it was very demanding. The work was hard, mistakes must not be made, trust and interdependence were essential, and no one worked in a vacuum. A good sailor must think laterally, be competent in many areas and able to cope with tensions, gossip and discomfort.

As a cadet, Raja said, he'd endured kicks but they'd made him a man and taught him self-discipline. In the days before he left home, tension set in. When he said goodbye to his family, it was for months or years at a time. Once it was for three years. When he returned, his son called him Uncle. His wife said, 'That's not Uncle that's Daddy.'

I liked his soft quick voice, his thoughtfulness and swanky, capable frame. I was surprised he was only twenty-six, for he seemed so wise. He came from Vellore. I asked what Salman's punishment would be. He said there'd be some loss of privileges and an obstacle to promotion, but that he was an immature young man who had much to learn. 'You mustn't make such mistakes on a ship,' he said. But Captain Dutt had said losing the keys was punishment enough.

I thought how punishing Bligh was to Christian at Nomuka when islanders stole the anchor of his boat, and how he humiliated him over the coconut affair. And then, on Sunday Island, when Robert Lamb was starving, Bligh beat him for eating the birds he'd caught.

That evening, though the officers had fish curry, Agnelo Dias, the cook from Goa, prepared Chicken Maryland with chips, a frizzed spring onion and sculpted carrot for Lady Myre and me. But he must have thought his efforts bland, for he poured curry sauce over it all. Pandal brought us each a glass of sweet white wine, and at our appreciation of so much kindness Dutt, Da Silva, Harminder, Raja and Soni all beamed.

Da Silva showed how he could cut an apple into flowery shapes. A restored Lady Myre made them all laugh when, with her rather beautiful hands, she cut orange peel into protruding teeth. She wore a silver leather miniskirt, a bust-bursting crimson top and a plastic daffodil in her hair. There was no coherence about her attire beyond it always looking odd. She never wore the same thing twice. One afternoon I saw her come from the engine room in combat gear and a deerstalker, and after Da Silva passingly remarked, one lunchtime, that as chief engineer he checked the air-conditioning to safeguard against legionnaires' disease, at dinner Lady Myre wore a mask with a carbon filter. She lifted it to speak and pop morsels of highly spiced food into her mouth. Da Silva appeared a little in love with her blondeness and insanity.

Sometimes she'd wear large diamond earrings that looked like trinkets, or flash a white sapphire ring, or she'd be festooned in sparkling beads from a Cairo street market.

Officers and crew all called her ma'am. I avoided calling her by any name, though in my mind I thought of her as Lady Myre. From her passport I'd seen that her first name was Hortense and that she was fifty-five. She told Captain Dutt she was forty but, as he had care of her passport, I wondered why she attempted this deception.

I thought of the defining details of name, date of birth, country of origin, and of the negating of the Polynesian women abducted by the mutineers. The men gave them English names: Isabella, Mary, Sarah, Jenny, Susannah, Nancy. Even their names were controlled by the sailors who abducted them, had sex with them, made them pregnant and whom they were obliged to serve. Bligh's descriptions of the mutineers made it hard to see them as romantic or attractive, with their sweaty hands, rotten teeth and scars. I tried to remember the girls' Polynesian names: Mauatua, Vahineatua, Teatuahitea... Their views on losing their homes, families, friends, and customs were not recorded. Caught in a crude adventure of crime and evasion, chance changed their lives beyond their control.

A rhythm of habits defined shipboard life: times to eat, the time when the water was hot enough for a bath, when the sun rose, when it set. I felt the persuasiveness of living for months and years on a ship, close to the circling of the world, the pull of the moon on the tide, the movement of the ocean bed. The ship was an island with only the sea in view. Some nights I went alone to the bridgehead deck to look at the stars and the moon's reflection in the ocean. I didn't want my voyage to end.

The crew seemed glad to have women on board, even women as odd as Lady Myre and me. Soni scolded them in Hindi when they flirted with Lady Myre.

For Saturday lunch Pandal served vegetarian curry, because of Soni's gods. Harminder told him it was horrible, Da Silva asked for luncheon meat to eat with it and Lady Myre spilled a forkful of hers down her shalwar-kameez, then dabbed the bright stain with a lemon. The talk was of marriage. Soni's had been arranged and she said how happy she was with her parents' choice of Jaswinder from Jamshedpur. She commended their wisdom and care. They asked for more from relationship than the frailty of falling in love. They wanted the good father, the good provider, and relatives they liked. Jaswinder sat beside her and looked inscrutable.

Da Silva said his was a love marriage and he'd want his children to choose for themselves in the same way he had. He'd tell them if he thought they were choosing unwisely, but he wouldn't deny them their freedom. Lady Myre expounded on meeting Sir Roland on Riis Beach and how it had been love at first sight. She said that love conquered all, then snapped her fingers for Pandal to bring more chapattis. Da Silva called her a true Christian and again said if ever she was in Mumbai she must stay at his house.

With a motive I didn't understand she then teased me with direct questions, wanting me to be embarrassed. What did I

think about love? Was there a man in *my* life? Did I have a significant other? I said I still hadn't found the love I was looking
for. She asked if I thought I'd find it on this journey. Captain
Dutt laughed. Soni said she thought it wrong that two lone
women were going to Pitcairn Island without the protection of
a husband or a brother, and Da Silva agreed.

In the afternoon Soni showed me her embroidered fabrics
and devotional paintings of her guru, husband and Krishna,
her shrine of holy relics, her photographs of the voyage. I
thought again of the women abducted on the *Bounty*, how they
must have yearned for home, without even a snapshot to console them.

22

For months Christian circled the Society, Cook and Friendly
Islands. He hoped to find the lost isles of Solomon as a place
to hide. He had a ship, crew, maps, charts, women and supplies, but no freedom to stop at any inhabited island.

Near Raratonga he bartered a piece of iron for a pig brought
out to the ship by a man in a canoe. The man returned to his
tribe to tell of the sight he'd seen: white-faced men and
strange animals on a floating island that arrived from
nowhere and where fresh water flowed and sugar cane grew.
Other tribesmen went to the ship to barter coconuts and
bananas. A boy stole a box of oranges. Another touched the
pearl buttons on Christian's jacket. On impulse Christian took
off the jacket and gave it to him. The boy stood on the gunwale
and displayed his prize. A mutineer shot him dead. The boy's

friends hauled his body from the sea then raced to the shore, shouting with shock and fear.

Bligh's command of the *Bounty* had been tight and focused. Now the ship was lawless. It buffeted where the wind took it. Its crew were unpredictable. Its boatmen explored whatever islands came into view. At Vatoa they caught birds and fish and picked up coconuts from the beach but when they saw people, pariahs as they were, they retreated to the ship and sailed on with the wind.

The Polynesians on board knew that *Bounty* was a misnomer, Christian a liar, and that they'd not meet again with Captain Cook or Bligh. The six young Polynesian men were called blacks by the mutineers and not given equal shares of food or comfort. No reckoning was made of the resentment this caused. Their expertise was needed for navigation and the lore of the islands. Two of them, Titahiti and Oheu, were from Tubuai, brothers of Chief Taroatehoa who'd ruled the district where Christian tried to build Fort George. Of the other four, Tararo was from the island of Raitea, two hundred miles north-west of Tahiti, and Teimua, Manarii and Niau were from Tahiti.

The twelve young women trapped on this voyage to isolation were in their early teens. One had a baby girl. They'd been taken for sex, to cook, serve and produce children in Christian's secret society. He called his woman Isabella. Her Polynesian name was Mauatua and she was the daughter of a Tahitian chief, from the *raatira* – the landed gentry. So was the woman/girl claimed by Edward Young. He called her Susan-

88

nah though her given name was Teraura. She was thirteen when she was taken from home. She had dark curly hair and was still growing. Bligh described Young as from a good family. Young's uncle, Sir George Young, had recommended his nephew to Bligh to sail with the *Bounty*.

The most vocal of the women, Teehuteatuaonoa, was called Jenny by the mutineers. Her ambition was to get home to Tahiti. She achieved this thirty-one years later in 1811. Her version of events was transcribed by a Captain Dillon and published in 1829. She was paired up with 'reckless Jack', a workhouse boy from Hackney, who'd run off to sea. He'd deserted from another ship to join the *Bounty* under the alias of Alexander Smith. On Pitcairn Island he again changed his name – to John Adams.

The rest of the women were shared among the mutineers and the Polynesian men, with the rule that the mutineers' desires took precedence. The two most feared men in the group, William McCoy and Matthew Quintal, both volunteers with the *Bounty*, were sexually violent when drunk.

23

In my cabin I read the account of Pitcairn that inspired Christian to go there. He'd found it in Bligh's copy of Hawksworth's *Voyages* and it was by an Englishman Captain Philip Carteret. 'It appeared like a great rock rising out of the sea. It was not more than five miles in circumference and seemed to be uninhabited.'

'Uninhabited' was the word Christian needed to see: no

prior possession, no fights for displacement, no massacre like on Tubuai.

'It was however covered with trees and we saw a small stream of fresh water running down one side of it.'

Water meant life: meat, vegetables, fruit, wood for houses, furniture, fences, boats, the opportunity to cultivate the seeds and plants he'd brought on the *Bounty*.

'I would have landed upon it but the surf broke upon it with great violence, and rendered this impossible. I got soundings on the west side of it, at somewhat less than a mile from the shore, in twenty-five fathoms, with a bottom of coral and sand. It is probable that in fine summer weather landing there may be practicable.'

This told Christian that were he to approach the island around December or January, unloading might be possible. And after that – no hostile ship could easily seek him out.

'We saw a great number of sea birds hovering about it at somewhat less than a mile from the shore and the sea seemed to have fish.'

So there'd be a larder: fish, eggs, clams, oysters. All the necessary food for survival, and delicacies too.

'It lies in latitude 20°2' south and longitude 133°21' west. It is so high that we saw it at the distance of more than fifteen leagues and it having been discovered by a young gentleman, son to Major Pitcairn of the marines, we called it Pitcairn Island.'

Christian knew these readings were wrong on every chart and that such an error might mean safety for him. Bligh had told him how he and Cook searched for the island in the *Res-*

olution in 1776, then gave up and sought respite in Tahiti because many of the crew had scurvy. The Polynesians with Christian on the *Bounty* calculated it lay 180 sea miles south-east from where Carteret had said.

Christian sighted Pitcairn Island on the evening of 15 January 1790, four months after leaving Tahiti. He saw this great rock rising from the sea, with clouds trapped above its mountain peaks. He and a well-armed crew took a boat to the shore. For two days he explored. He found all he'd hoped for. No people, no hospitable bay for a ship of retribution to anchor, a rugged coast, inland forests of coconut palms, breadfruit, miro and hibiscus trees, nesting birds, freshwater springs and flat land for building. The bays were full of fish, and oysters clung to the rocks.

He returned to the *Bounty* 'with a joyful expression such as we had not seen on him for a long time past'. He'd found what he was looking for, what he thought would save him, an island to colonise, a world to control, as far away from Bligh and the gallows as the earth could provide.

24

The sky was dark and starless on the night the *Tundra Princess* approached Pitcairn. Again there was driving rain and waves twenty-six feet high. The ship sounded its horn each minute, an eerie bellow. On the bridgehead Captain Dutt said that unless there was improvement soon, he wouldn't stop. His scalp jiggled, his eyes looked anxious. He faxed his company. They again warned him not to anchor, for the ship might swing. Again he said his priority was his ten-million-dollar cargo of kiwi fruit.

The island appeared as a bright speck on the radar screen. Lady Myre asked questions about how radar worked. Captain Dutt's answers were terse. A fax came from Pitcairn's mayor, Steve Christian, telling him not to try to approach until dawn. He should then go to the lee of the island, where the sea was calmer, and drift until the longboats came to unload supplies and collect Lady Myre and me. It would be three miles back to Adamstown, the only settlement, but the swell was too great to attempt to unload near Bounty Bay.

Dutt told Lady Myre and me to pack our bags, leave them in our cabins, then come to the bridge at dawn. He reduced the ship's speed to fifteen knots. 'Why do you want to go to this benighted place?' he asked. 'I don't understand it. Don't you have family? It's not necessary.' I thought of the migration of swallows, the restless travel of people, the transport of kiwi fruit, the feeding of Tahitian breadfruit to West Indian slaves. I wondered what was necessary.

For our last supper we had mutton and cabbage. The talk was of the war in Iraq, how wrong it was, how unsafe it made us feel. 'It should not have happened,' Da Silva said, and Harminder, Jaswinder and Captain Dutt agreed. Lady Myre said we had to fight to preserve civilisation, but no one took any notice of her. She and Soni and Da Silva then took photographs of us all with their digital cameras, and we exchanged email addresses and invitations to our homes. Soni gave Lady Myre an assortment of glittering stars and spots to stick round her nose and eyes, and me a necklace of wooden beads. Lady

Myre then went to the lounge to watch a video of *The Sound of Music* with Da Silva. I returned to my cabin to pack and prepare to land.

At six in the morning, the *Tundra Princess* idled three miles offshore from Pitcairn in a turbulent sea. The clouds were black and there was driving rain. Wrapped in waterproofs, Lady Myre and I stood in a haze of wet, with our wallets, passports, tickets and liquor licences concealed in our bum bags. Pandal had put our luggage – my rucksack, her fourteen motley cases and boxes – in thick blue polythene bags.

Captain Dutt looked through binoculars at the island's gloom. 'I don't like this,' he said. 'I don't like the look of those rocks.' He repeated that he could not linger and that it would not be possible to unload supplies. 'They're coming,' he said and handed me the binoculars. He made it sound interplanetary. I saw a longboat filled with people, most of them in yellow oilskins. The boat rose to the crest of each wave, then plunged from view. Lady Myre looked too. 'Whoosh!' she said, and then again, 'Whoosh! Is it coming to collect us? What a heck of a lark.' She faltered and gave her wide, toothy smile. 'But how do we get into it?' she asked. 'How do we get off this ship and into that bucketing tub?'

'Do exactly as you're told,' Dutt replied. 'I'll give you gloves so the rope doesn't burn your hands.'

'Rope?' she said. 'What do you mean, rope?'

'The rope of the ladder,' Dutt said.

'But you will put the gangway down for us so that we can alight from the ship to the boat.'

'You would end up in the sea,' he said.

Her smile switched off. 'I am Lady Myre,' she said, the fright of it all reminding her of her class. 'I am not a chimpanzee.'

'I am concerned for you,' said Captain Dutt. 'This is folly. Why do you want to go to this terrible place? You should come with us to Panama. This is not a civilised place to leave a lady such as yourself. Your husband would be most disconcerted. He should not allow it.'

Perhaps aware that he had crossed a cultural barrier of opinion, his scalp jiggled and he said no more. Other officers, in uniform, assembled to wish us luck and say goodbye. Another longboat came into view, it roller-coasted with each wave. The men in both boats stood tall, spray burst over them, they disappeared then appeared again. As they manoeuvred alongside the ship, the boats looked like specks against this huge vessel of 17,000 tons. I thought of the nineteen men, cast adrift from the *Bounty* in a cutter. Ropes were thrown and caught and the Jacob's ladder lowered. Several Pitcairners effortlessly climbed up it. I observed how strong they were, how physical. I did not see how I or Lady Myre could find our descent easy.

Steve Christian was first on deck. Barefoot and wearing shorts, with a knife at his belt and a T-shirt with a Pitcairn logo, he was drenched with seawater and rain. He walked with a limp. One of his legs, broken when he was a boy, was shorter than the other. He was thick-built, dark-haired, darkskinned. I thought of Bligh's description of Fletcher Christian:

'5 feet 9 inches high, blackish or very dark complexion, dark brown hair, strong made'.

He took no notice of Lady Myre or me. He asked Captain Dutt if he had alcohol or cigarettes to sell. His voice was sing-song, polite. Dutt said that he did not. I thought of the prohibitions of Adventism. Steve then asked Dutt if he'd use the ship's cranes to unload the island's supplies from the containers. Most of these supplies were building materials for the new prison and there was no way they could be shifted by hand. I thought how Steve was the main defendant in the sex-abuse trials and that the prison was for him. Dutt said to raise the cranes in this weather would jeopardise the stability of the ship and he wasn't prepared to risk it.

Bea Christian joined Steve. She was a cousin of sorts and looked like him. She too was barefoot, dressed in shorts and T-shirt and drenched with rain and spray. She too had a knife at her belt. They shook hands with Lady Myre and me and said, 'Welcome to Pitcairn,' but there was reserve in their eyes. I thought of the far-back mother from whom they'd once come, Mauatua, Fletcher Christian's Isabella, lured from Tahiti, caught in his crime.

They went to the container deck to unload what they could by hand. I waited on the bridgehead with Lady Myre. 'Gosh,' she said, her eyes bewildered, her smile white and wide, 'I didn't think it would be quite like this.'

As the morning lightened, we more clearly saw the outline of the island and the fierceness of the sea. 'It's crazy,' Da Silva said. 'We won't see you again. They have knives and no shoes.

She is not a woman. Look at her muscles.' But then he said, as if to belie the words he'd just spoken, 'What an adventure. Imagine the mutineers arriving here. I wish I was going with you.'

'You must come to Panama,' said Captain Dutt with terrible consistency. I knew little about Panama. It was not my choice of destination, least of all with Lady Myre. I'd heard it was a centre for money-laundering and cocaine shipment, and that forty per cent of its population lived in poverty, which led to opportunistic crime.

We moved to the container deck. It was awash. Islanders struggled to lower supplies into the longboats: sodden and disintegrating cardboard boxes of onions, potatoes, meat and eggs, a bag of mail, building planks, cylinders of gas and drums of petrol. They covered this muddle of saturated goods with green tarpaulin.

They seemed dejected, inured. Bea was the only woman among them. They spoke only occasionally in sing-song pidgin and didn't look at Lady Myre or me. I asked a large man with a protruding lower lip, his eyes lost in fat, how we'd get into the boat.

'I'll catch you with one hand,' he said, and laughed. 'But when I say "Now", let go the rope. If you don't, you'll be caught between the ship and the boat. There's only a moment before the next wave.'

Lady Myre was sober. 'I can't swing from that trapeze,' she said. 'I'm not a stunt artiste. I am – ' She slid across the deck and shrieked.

I tried to console her. 'Think of it as a live performance,' I said. 'You must get it right. Imagine the whole world's watching you and do as you're told.'

I doubted she had a history of doing as she was told.

The first boat lurched away with its sodden cargo. I said my last goodbyes to our Indian friends who seemed quiet and dignified.

The Pitcairners exclaimed as Lady Myre's luggage was lowered. It filled much of the second boat. She then braved the ladder, gripped it hard and froze.

'Now!' the fat man called.

She clung on tight, a wave washed over her, he pushed the boat clear of her legs.

'Now!' he called again.

Another wave hit her.

'This is not right,' Captain Dutt said. 'This is very wrong.'

'Now!' the fat man called. 'Now, now, now!'

She spread to horizontal, her legs and arms splayed. A Pitcairn man caught and righted her. She whooped and smiled and dripped with wet. 'It's wonderful,' she called up to me. 'Like bungee jumping.'

I made my leap of faith. The fat man caught me like a leaf. The side of the *Tundra Princess* looked unscalable from the boat. The sea was deafening. Steve fired the outboard motor. The prow thwacked against the waves, surf broke over us. 'Yes!' exclaimed Lady Myre at every impact. I clung to a rowlock to keep my balance and waved to the Indian crew. The ship looked like a land mass, a destination. I thought of the astonished eighteenth-century Polynesians when the *Bounty* appeared on the empty sea. I observed the charcoal of the sky, the roar of the sea, the taste of salt, the sharpness of the air, the size and whiteness of the ship, the still cluster of uniformed men on the deck, the widening space between the ship and the boat. The word 'goodbye' was in my heart. I waved and waved. I thought of Bligh in that crowded boat as he watched the *Bounty* sail away, of Verity blowing a kiss as I went through the departure gate, of a far-back image of an elderly man in a black coat on a forgotten jetty, waving at someone I didn't know, who was on the same ship as I. He waved and waved. As the ship pulled away he became a speck. He ran down the jetty, took out a white handkerchief, and waved some more.

We rounded Pitcairn to the south of the island where the sea was too wild for the *Tundra Princess*. The longboat cracked against waves. I shivered with cold and wiped salt water from my eyes. 'With unremitting violence', as Carteret said, the surf crashed against the cliff face. Frigate birds swooped low, coconut palms crested the cliff tops, clouds were trapped in the mountains. I thought of the apprehension of the women on the *Bounty* as they drew near to this harsh place so unlike their home.

A cluster of people came into view on the small, rough-hewn jetty at Bounty Bay. They'd been waiting since dawn, scanning the sea, knowing its power. A wave rushed the boat to the landing place. Ropes were thrown and seized. Hands hauled us to the land. Islanders anxiously enquired about the hoped-for provisions. Lady Myre and I were scrutinised. She

looked dazed and was unnaturally quiet. A scattering of children stared. Someone introduced us cursorily to the group,
most of whom were 'visitors' from New Zealand: a teacher,
two social workers, two prison-builders, a locum and his wife,
the governor's representative and his wife, two policemen
from Britain.

I'd arrived at my chosen destination no matter how random
the reasons for choosing it. With all that voyaging there was
now no turning back. '*Hello*,' Rosie Christian said with a relief
and smile I echoed. 'So glad you've made it. In this terrible
weather, all this way and after all this time.' I sensed her kindness, that common bond, and I realised, with disappointment,
that I'd made a mistake in my choice of blouse.

III

ON PITCAIRN

*The interplay of different rhythms produces a special
version of chaos*

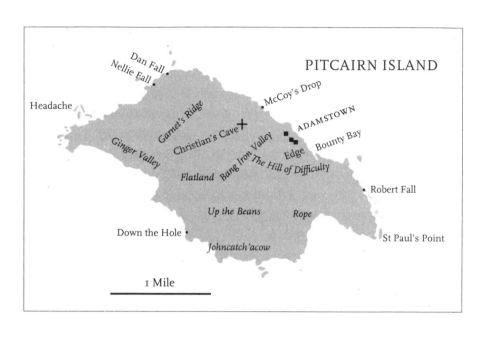

PITCAIRN ISLAND

Dan Fall
Nellie Fall
Headache
McCoy's Drop
Garnet's Ridge
ADAMSTOWN
Christian's Cave
Ginger Valley
Bang Iron Valley
Edge
Bounty Bay
Flatland
The Hill of Difficulty
Up the Beans
Rope
Robert Fall
Down the Hole
St Paul's Point
Johncatch'acow

1 Mile

25

Bligh returned to England in March 1790 to a swathe of publicity. He'd been away two years. His account of the mutiny was unequivocal. He told Sir Joseph Banks he'd have had to be 'more than human' to have foreseen what happened. 'To the last I never lost that presence of mind or professional skill which you have been pleased to allow was the first cause of my being honoured with your notice... My Character & Honor is Spotless,' he wrote. 'My Conduct has been free of blame.' He said if he'd had commissioned officers and trained marines, 'most likely the affair would never have happened. I had not a spirited or brave fellow about me.'

He singled out Fletcher Christian and Peter Heywood as the main culprits. He'd every day

rendered them some service ... It is incredible! These very young Men I placed every confidence in, yet these great Villains joined with the most able men in the ship, got possession of the Arms and took the *Bounty* from me with Huzzas for Otaheite. I have now every reason to curse the day I ever knew a Christian or a Heywood.

Bligh capitalised on his ordeal. On 1 April the *London Chronicle* advertised publication of *Captain Bligh's Journal of his Wonderful Escape at Sea in an Open Boat for 49 Days*. George Nicol, 'Bookseller to His Majesty', published the first part with the title *A Narrative of the Mutiny on Board His Majesty's Ship* Bounty; *and the Subsequent Voyage of Part of the Crew in the Ship's Boat from Tofua, one of the Friendly Islands, to Timor, a Dutch Settlement in the East Indies.* A sequel, published anonymously, promised 'Secret Anecdotes of the

Otaheitean Women Whose Charms it is thought Influenced the Pirates in the Commission of the Daring Conspiracy'. At the Royalty Theatre, there was a sell-out musical *The Pirates, Or the Calamities of Captain Bligh*. Ralph Wewitzer starred as Bligh and Miss Daniels sang 'Loose Ev'ry Sail'. A less successful musical followed, *Tar Against Perfume or The Sailor Preferred*.

Neither Heywood's mother nor his sister Nessy believed their Peter could be guilty of mutiny or dishonour. He'd been fifteen when he joined the *Bounty*. Mrs Heywood wrote an imploring, desperate letter to Bligh on behalf of her son. Bligh's reply was nasty:

Madam
I received your Letter this Day & feel for you very much, being perfectly sensible of the extreme Distress you must suffer from the Conduct of your Son Peter. His baseness is beyond all Description, but I hope you will endeavour to prevent the Loss of him, heavy as the misfortune is, from afflicting you too severely. I imagine he is, with the rest of the Mutineers, returned to Otaheite.

The Admiralty authorised a frigate, the *Pandora*, with twenty-four guns and 160 men, under the command of Captain Edward Edwards, to seek out the mutineers. Edwards was to sail first to Tahiti, and if the men weren't there, or only some of them, he was to call at the Society and Friendly Islands and other islands in the Pacific to round up as many of the 'delinquents' as he could discover. 'You are', his orders read, 'to keep the mutineers as closely confined as may preclude all possibility of their escaping, that they may be brought home to undergo the punishment due to their demerits.'

That punishment was hanging. Article 19 of the Naval Articles of War was unambiguous. 'If any person in or belonging to the fleet shall make or endeavour to make any mutinous assembly upon any pretence whatsoever, every person offending herein and being convicted thereof by the sentence of the court-martial shall suffer DEATH.'

Edwards was also to fulfil the ancillary task that had been assigned to Bligh: 'To survey the Endeavour Straits to facilitate the passage of vessels to Botany Bay'.

Bligh's own court martial for the loss of the *Bounty* was a necessary formality. It was held on board HMS *Royal William* at Spithead on 22 October before Admiral Samuel Barrington and eleven captains. Asked by the court if he had 'objection or complaint' against any of the men who survived the open-boat journey, Bligh said he had none, except minor instances of impudence and non-compliance from Purcell the carpenter. In turn, under cross-examination, all the men swore they'd no objection or complaint concerning Bligh, they'd known nothing of the mutiny before it occurred and they'd done everything in their power to recover the ship. John Fryer, the master, kept quiet about his loathing of Bligh. He said he'd tried to reason with Christian as he held a bayonet over Bligh, whose hands were tied, and that Christian had told him to hold his tongue and said he'd been in hell for a week. Midshipman John Hallett described how Bligh was held at knifepoint, 'naked all to his shirt and night cap', and how his servant 'was ordered to go below for his trowsers and to haul them on for him'.

The testimony was consistent and the court concluded that 'the *Bounty* was violently and forcibly seized by the said Fletcher Christian and certain other mutineers'. They honourably acquitted Lieutenant Bligh, and those tried with him, of responsibility for her loss. The only punishment meted out was a reprimand to Purcell for not complying with orders while on Tahiti: refusing to hoist water out of the ship's hold when instructed to do so and refusing to cut a grinding stone for one of the chiefs.

Cleared of all wrongdoing, Bligh was extolled as a hero and officially promoted. He remained on full pay from the Admiralty from the time of his return until the trial. He was presented to King George the Third who asked how his cheek had come to be scarred. Bligh told him it was from a childhood accident when his father, in their orchard in Plymouth, had thrown a hatchet at a horse to try to make it turn so that he could catch it.

On 7 February 1791 Bligh put in an expenses claim to the Admiralty of £283/1/6d for possessions lost with the *Bounty*. This included £47/0/6d for his personal books and charts, £121/12/od for his clothes, and £59/13/6d for liquor. On 15 April he set sail in HMS *Providence* with another Admiralty commission to take breadfruit from Tahiti to Britain's starving slaves in the West Indies. This time he had the rank and pay of captain.

26

Rosie stayed at the jetty to help unload the island's sodden supplies. Smiley took me up the Hill of Difficulty on his quad bike. I gripped the seat and my polythene-covered bag. Red mud splattered as Murray had warned. Beyond the noise of the bike and the swirling rain was the stillness of the land after the turbulent sea. There was a tropical warmth, though this was Pitcairn's winter.

Smiley had been three months on the island, supervising the building of the prison. He wanted to finish and go home to Christchurch, but now the required wood and materials and the perimeter fence were bound for Panama. 'Here it is.' He stopped his bike by what looked like a Swiss chalet. 'The guys who stand to be holed up in it are building it with me. Now there's nothing for them to do. It won't ever be finished on time.'

It was a smart building in tongue-and-groove, with a deck round it and individual front doors to what I supposed were the six cells. 'It's really nice,' Smiley said, with a good workman's pride. 'Each unit's got its own shower, basin, urinal and power points. It's all built to EEC standards. It's much better than the Pitcairners' houses.'

I asked why the defendants had agreed to build it, as if digging their own graves.

'It's good money,' he said. 'They figure if they don't get it, some outsider will. The British government pays. Anyway, they won't ever be banged up in it, they'll get off on a technicality. And even if they do get sent down, they'll be allowed out to work the longboats and go fishing and whatever. The island can't manage without them.'

Prison warders were to be brought from New Zealand to supervise them. 'It'll cost,' he said, 'they'll have to charter a ship, and then there's accommodation for them and food and everything.'

It all seemed bizarre. He then talked about quad bikes – how they were the only transport and the only possible way to get over Pitcairn's rough terrain. He said they were inherently unstable and going down hill in the rain, with the wheels all caked with mud, was a gas. He knew how to pull a wheelie and loop the loop, but he wouldn't show me right now.

We drove on. 'That's October Christian's house' – he waved at a derelict shed. 'He was Fletcher Christian's son and guess when he was born. That's the shop' – he waved again. 'It's open Tuesdays and Thursdays for an hour. That's the church, that's the school, that's the post office and that's the courthouse.' Then we stopped outside a low-built wooden house. 'And that's about it really. That's Pitcairn. You wait here till Rosie arrives. I've got to taxi more stuff. Nice to meet you. Bye.'

I stood among ferns and coconut palms. Beyond the house was a tangle of banana trees, passion fruit and yams. Bees buzzed round hives. The sky had changed to blue in an instant. Semi-feral cats scampered to a safe distance then sat and watched, hoping I'd provide food. The front door was open and I looked into a hallway stuffed with coats, boxes, boots, baskets, papers, tools, spades, sticks, bottles, all tinged with red mud. I felt alarm, for I like to live in an orderly way. I realised I equated island life with simplicity and an absence of possessions. At the side of the house was a mass of washing hanging under a tin awning. A wood fire burned between stones to heat a blackened tank from which pipes ran into the house.

Another quad bike, top-heavy with Lady Myre's luggage, drew up driven by Ed the Scottish policeman. His accent was broad and I wondered if the Pitcairners managed to understand him. As he unloaded her cases and boxes, he said he was leaving next time the *Braveheart*, the government chartered transport ship, called. He'd done three months' community policing on the island and he too wanted to go home.

Lady Myre arrived on Rosie's bike. She was clutching her round the waist and had wrapped her feet in bin bags. She looked bedraggled and her pizzazz had deserted her.

'What's my luggage doing here?' she said. 'I told them to take it straight to my hotel.'

'What hotel's that?' Rosie asked.

'The Beachcomber, Waikawa,' Lady Myre said.

'I don't know what this is about,' said Rosie. 'There's no hotel on Pitcairn.'

'My agent booked it from Kensington.' Lady Myre sounded frosty. 'With a sea view and my own jacuzzi.'

'It's a room in my house or a room in Suzanne's house,' Rosie said. 'Shirley must have told you that in Auckland. Thirty-five dollars a night including breakfast and dinner. Fifty if you want all the tours and a midday picnic.'

'I don't know any Shirley,' Lady Myre said, and I wondered

again about her mental state. 'There's a misunderstanding. I've a reservation at the Beachcomber.'

A black cloud scudded into the blue sky and again there was a sudden and terrific deluge of rain. 'Come inside,' Rosie said. 'It's here or here. It's my house or the rain. There ain't no hotel or jacuzzi on Pitcairn.'

27

A mile offshore from Pitcairn Fletcher Christian ordered that the *Bounty* be emptied and stripped. Everything of conceivable use was unloaded to the boats, then to a raft made from the ship's hatches and hauled by ropes. Animals, wood, plants, books, gold ducats, hammocks, rum, wine – all were dragged to the stony beach where no boat could moor. The contents of the ship and the produce of the island were all these colonisers would have. Armaments, the cannon, knives, axes, tools, masts, the forge, sails, yardages, tinder boxes, compasses, fishing gear – all were carried up the Hill of Difficulty to the Edge, a flat bit of land overlooking what they called Bounty Bay.

The mood of the community was of factional resentment and deep distrust. Even while Christian was reconnoitring the island John Mills had tried to persuade the others to sail off to Tahiti and leave him stranded without supplies. Christian wanted to keep the ship's bare hull. The others suspected he'd refurbish it, move on and maroon the rest of them, so on 23 January 1790, less than a week after their arrival, Matthew Quintal torched it. He was vengeful towards Christian, who on Tubuai had accused him of mutiny and drunkenness, threatened him with a pistol and put him in irons. The women wept as they watched the *Bounty* burn. Into the flames went their chance of returning home.

Christian warned all those with him that death would be the penalty for trying to escape. They were to be invisible to passing ships. At first they all camped in tents made from sailcloth. Goats, pigs and hens were let loose to multiply. Melons, plantains, sweet potatoes, arrowroot, bananas and yams were planted. William Brown, who'd trained at the Royal Botanical Gardens at Kew, had the practical skills to establish crops. Edward Young kept a journal, subsequently lost, in which he wrote of building houses, fencing in and cultivating gardens, fishing, catching birds and cooking Polynesian fashion on hot stones in the ground.

The mutineers – the 'whites' – divided the entire island's usable land among themselves and claimed all its fishing points. Each took a woman for his own use. The six Polynesian men – the 'blacks' – were denied any rights. They were used as slaves, like the West Indians who might have been the recipients of the breadfruit cargo. Their food was not as choice, they inhabited inferior quarters, were beaten if they disobeyed and accorded only the three women not wanted by their masters.

Their indigenous expertise was needed, though: for building, farming and dyeing cloth, for identifying edible plants and fruits. They knew the disposition of the seasons, the lore of the weather, the habits of birds and fish. They were the architects of the wooden houses, which were double-storeyed, rectangular and thatched with palm branches laced to rafters. One side was removable in hot weather. Downstairs was the living and eating area. A trapdoor and ladder led to the bedroom.

They were afflicted and traduced and they had two options: to build a boat and sail away on a moonlit night when the sea was calm, or to murder their oppressors.

28

There was a room each for Lady Myre and me. I conceded that the larger must be hers. It had a chest of drawers, patterned lino, a bedspread with red lilies on it, an array of teddy bears wrapped in cellophane on a pelmet above a small window. By the time we'd brought in all her luggage there was no room to move.

Rosie went back to the jetty to help sort more stuff. I put my rucksack in my room. There was a bare bulb above a single bed and on the wall a framed print of a bearded saint and magazine cut-outs of three puppies and two cats. I turned down the floral sheet, peered at the mattress and feared its history. There was a pink net curtain at the window and a chair with yellow stuffing coming out of it. I fixed a hook in the ceiling above the bed, hung my mosquito net, sprayed the room and myself with mosquito repellent, sprinkled bug powder in the bed and in my silk sleeping bag, put purifying tablets into my water bottle and arranged my neat possessions: a black notebook, my Pelikan pencil, Swiss army knife, compass, camera, travel clock. I opened the window and looked out on a tangle of fallen branches and terns that swirled and swooped. There was the hum of insects and the sound of sawing timber, perhaps from the building of the prison.

I explored the house. Lady Myre had assumed a jacuzzi and room service. I'd anticipated tranquil simplicity: crude wood structures and vernal beauty. I'd overlooked a basic Pitcairn rule: discard nothing. All the grunge of human life was stored. Everything might have a lateral use: broken freezers, boxes that once contained soap powder, tins that once contained beans, empty sacks, bottles and plastic tubs, bubble-wrap, flex, cardboard, sticks, broken chairs, carpet remnants, glass, magazines, building boards – all of it might come in handy one day. And then there were all the provisions because the ship of plenty might never arrive: sacks of flour, cartons of everlasting milk, freezers filled with food that froze and thawed and froze and thawed. Sell-by dates were a foible of another place. Self-sufficiency meant anticipating every eventuality.

The house was unfinished, though its basic structure was intact. Doors, banisters, dowelling, railing for an upper terrace might all perhaps one day arrive. There was a bucket to catch the rainwater that came through the roof, flexes that trailed to ham radios, fans, fires. There were stacks of Pitcairn T-shirts, woven baskets, and carved wooden curios of dolphins and the *Bounty* to sell to passengers if and when the cruise ship came.

Everything was a habitat for some creature. Cats and kittens shot through. Cockroaches paraded in dark corners. Small retiring beasts scuffled in the storage and left their marks. Black, noiseless, indigenous mosquitoes sucked new blood undeterred by Deet. There was an oppressive humidity even in what passed as winter, a wet, fusty-smelling heat, loved by insects and rodents and which made mould grow.

Back in my room I felt dejected. The mutineers and Polynesian settlers had gone from my mind. I thought how buildings insulate us and how I wanted to impose my own marks and style and usurp all other occupants of this space.

Lady Myre came in with the hypodermics and flu vaccines Captain Dutt had entrusted to her. She asked if I'd ever been a user and if I thought whatever it was would get her through this. I took the vaccines from her and told her to have courage. She was all in white except for a scarlet headband. She eyed my mosquito net and asked if she might share my bed, because she was afraid of murder. I said I didn't think that was a good idea and we must try to adjust to the customs of the island. She said she was in a real pickle and did I think God had a reason for sending her to the end of nowhere. I said I thought not, but that she should've done her research better if she'd really wanted to go to Picton. 'You must've known,' I said. 'Enough people must've told you.' She made a strange sort of noise, as if blowing little kisses at me, and vowed she wasn't going to let me out of her sight. Fate had sent her not to Garth but to me.

Lady Myre was not the same person as had shimmered as she danced with Captain Dutt. Her eyes took on a vague look and she gazed towards the ocean in perhaps the way the abductees had gazed. 'You must tell Roley to send a ship,' she said.

I suggested she send an email, but it seemed he couldn't even configure the channels on a television, so there was scant hope of digital communication. I wondered about his navigational skills. I probed. He might not be staying in Little Nevish or Knightsbridge but in The Rookery, a hotel somewhere in London. I offered, while the electricity generator was still going and if Rosie agreed, to log on via her laptop to see if I could find such a place. I asked Lady Myre what message she'd like me to send.

'Say,' she said – and she became engrossed in the theatre of her predicament – 'say that Hortense has been deceived, taken captive to a terrible place, marooned on a barren Pacific island. Worse than Alcatraz.' Her blue eyes burned with the performance, her voice trembled. 'Worse than Rock or Robben Island. Worse than Spandau. In primitive quarters, denied all ordinary comfort and surrounded by child-molesters. Say he must send a ship for her.'

Rosie's laptop, an ancient Toshiba, was kept wrapped in a piece of blanket on a rickety table beneath a pile of papers. 'That's fine,' Rosie said about using it. 'Whenever you feel like it. There's no charge.'

I first emailed a message of safe arrival to Verity and my brothers and invited them to contact me if they wished, but to be circumspect because mail could be read. Prompted by Lady Myre, I then tried to communicate with the elusive Sir Roland. I found email addresses for six London Rookeries but she was unsure in which of them he might reside and said he could be on the Isle of Wight. I sent the same message to all six unlikely abodes:

To Whom It May Concern:

Would you please advise Sir Roland Myre that his wife Hortense has arrived on Pitcairn Island in the South Pacific. She is distressed and feels marooned. There is no shipping off the island and it has no airstrip. She wishes to be transported to more congenial territory and would appreciate it if, given his distinguished naval career and the high regard in which he holds her, he would arrange for a carrier to collect her.

'At the earliest,' said Lady Myre. 'Add "at the earliest".' 'At the earliest,' I wrote, and explained my details. I was confused as to why she didn't contact some mutual friend and I began to doubt whether Sir Roland existed, or if she was who she claimed to be, but her agitation was real. She was then restless in the long hours when the electricity generator wasn't working and unreceptive to my explanations about the need for patience over a reply, because of the rotating of the earth around the sun and people's need for sleep.

When Rosie returned from the jetty I gave her the watch and vaccines, then took courage and gave her the blouse. She made a gracious display of carefully unwrapping it from the tissue paper, then put it on and paraded and exclaimed. Hank and Lady Myre watched. It was abjectly wrong. Shiny and clinging, it revealed in all the unflattering places. I resisted apology for that would have prompted undeserved reassurance. Rosie said she'd wear it in church, and when she and Hank next went to America to visit Adventist missions. Verity had been right. Something ordinary for twenty pounds from Leather Lane would have served. Some large, dark, cotton garment that covered up. I'd tried too hard and I'd failed. Lady

Myre said it was smashing for a disco and was there one on the island? She then told a gushing anecdote about when she'd won second prize in salsa dancing at the Hackney Empire, wearing a tuxedo and silver slingbacks and smoking a fat Havana. Neither Hank nor Rosie knew what she was talking about and she gave the impression of being deranged.

On Rosie's quad bike we toured the island. All two square miles of it. We clung on and bumped down the mud tracks, through Adamstown – named after John Adams, who wasn't John Adams at all, or Alexander Smith as he'd previously called himself, but just another rogue who'd jumped ship, mutinied, murdered, and holed up on Pitcairn – along the Edge, past Big Fence and Down Side, past the courthouse and church, the *Bounty*'s anchor on a plinth, the governor's house, the cave at Garnet's Ridge where Fletcher Christian was said to have shut himself away and moped, past the old gaol and the satellite station. 'There's a phone in there,' Rosie shouted, above the noise of the bike. Lady Myre became agitated and insisted she must phone Sir Roland. Rosie said it was very expensive and she'd have to ask Wayne, the governor's representative, who was the only one with a key.

I had no clear sense of what was where and felt we were going round in circles. It was undoubtedly a rugged place of sheer cliffs, steep peaks and little valleys. The awfulness of it was a sense of being stuck. No ferry at dawn, no departures, arrivals, no journeys. I thought of my mother in residential care. No brave new world and such people in it.

Rosie stopped at one of her gardens, as the plots of land

inherited from ancestors were called, to gather oranges, lemons and grapefruit. There was the sweet sharp smell of citrus as in a timeless way we three women put fruit into baskets. I thought of the iniquity of not according gardens to the Polynesians, of the disparagement coded into the word 'blacks', of my resentment if I was treated as 'only a woman'. Again I imagined the anguish of the Polynesian women as they watched the *Bounty* burn.

As I chopped cabbage in Rosie's kitchen, I counted twenty-seven cats in the yard by the door. They scratched at fleas. Kittens flitted in and grabbed any food that fell to the floor. Tomcats sprayed. Each day Hank boiled a saucepan of rice for them all, in case they were the reincarnated souls of Christians. Most of them were orange or black-and-white. There was constant war between the island's cat and rat populations. When the feral cats were winning, Steve Christian, who was the island's engineer and dentist as well as the mayor, chased them with a chisel and chopped off their testicles. They'd drag themselves around for a while then recover. He did the same for the island's goats. When the rats overwhelmed, the islanders went on shooting sprees. On their best day Rosie and Hank shot fourteen hundred brown or black rats. Hank shot at one that looked as if it was praying by the roadside. He missed, and supposed it had been spared by the grace of God.

Rosie cracked a coconut on a spike and shredded its flesh. She prepared an enormous meal: green-banana pancakes, breadfruit patties, wild beans, nanwee fish, lamb baked in coconut milk, cabbage salad. Lady Myre said she was too upset to eat any of it, but changed her mind when Rosie told her nanwee was called the dream fish for its hallucinogenic properties and that her own mother, after eating it, would moan in her sleep and call out the names of long-dead ancestors.

Conversation moved naturally to the Resurrection and the Second Coming of Christ. When He arrived, the good would have eternal life and sinners would be damned, unless they repented and followed the cross. On a video, gospel singers swayed. Lady Myre sang along to 'Mine Eyes Have Seen the Glory of the Coming of the Lord'. I set the table and poured myself a glass of wine from my box of Spy Valley Pinot Noir. Discomfort registered on Rosie's face at the sight and smell of wine. Hank sat at the head of the formica table and graciously thanked God for providing our supper. Lady Myre warbled an extravagantly loud 'Amen'. Hank talked of the problems of shipping and the cost now that the island's supplies were heading towards Panama. Something scuttled beneath the table. I swatted my arms and ankles and ate a breadfruit patty. Lady Myre devoured a large quantity of the hallucinogenic fish. It seemed that Verity, my mother and all ambition were of the past and that there was no other world than here.

Though I was covered by the mosquito net and smothered in Deet, creatures from their home in the mattress still rose to eat me. I'd read that with a sticky bar of soap in hand, in a rapid movement one should throw back the covers, flash a light and zap these bugs. I did this and found not recognisable bed bugs but tiny creatures with lots of legs, dead on their backs.

A hand gripped my shoulder as I flashed and zapped. I screeched. She was an apparition in black satin, her face a white lanolin mask, her hair in a net. She'd fixed a sort of miner's lamp to her forehead. 'Help me,' she croaked. She said there was a puma in her room, that she was terrified and must share my bed. I told her it was too small and that there were bugs in it. She asked me to escort her to the lavatory. She'd looked in and there was a family of cockroaches around it – would I do something about them and wait with her while she spent a penny?

A car battery provided low-voltage orange light in the bathroom during the hours without electricity. I shooed away the roaches and waited with Lady Myre. She grizzled and keened. I offered to swap beds if that would make things better. She said she'd prefer my bed because of the net and the sprays. I wondered with all her luggage that she'd omitted a common-sense thing like a mosquito net. She wanted me to sleep in the bed with her because she said she'd never needed a cuddle more. I told her I didn't think that was a good idea. Then she wanted me to go with her, high up to Garnet's Ridge, to light a fire to attract some non-existent passing ship. I told her an islander might shoot us, for they all had guns. I chivalrously waited while she washed her hands, guided her to my room, sprayed her legs with repellent, arranged her under the net and promised to help her all I could.

Lying in Lady Myre's bed in the moonless dark, surrounded by all her boxes and cases, deprived of my neat possessions or hope of sleep, I tried to get some hold on my life. I thought of

Verity, our cool Egyptian-cotton sheets, the firm mattress, the wall of books, the cleanness of surfaces. Perhaps tomorrow I'd send her a message, 'The weather's changeable and humid. Had wild beans and green-banana pancakes for tea.'

I thought of my mother and the world she'd contrived because of some malevolent function of the cells in her brain, her constant search for possessions she believed stolen.

The sea, so often a consolation, was now a worry. It stretched for ever like an enclosing moat. I reminded myself that the remains of the *Bounty* were out there in the bay, ten feet under water. I could dive to see it. I tried to imagine that first haul up the Hill of Difficulty, through thick vegetation, the relief of surviving animals as they headed for the valleys and the hills, the urgency to build shelter, get water, cook food, the fear of discovery by some, the longing for it by others.

By an accident of circumstance I now inhabited the world of Lady Myre. New Zealand was three thousand miles away. I feared no ship would ever come. I wondered what would happen if she or I became ill or had a fall. She seemed a more pressing problem than rapists and child abusers. I worried about her being bitten under my net, what would be best for her and how to find a ship to take her to a congenial place.

Dispiritedly I thought of Rosie's blouse and my searching in all those shops. Endless choice and I'd bought the wrong thing. Something rustled under the bed. It was not, of course, a puma. It was probably a mouse or cat. The room had a warm, musty smell. And so the night wore on. Circles of thinking. The scuffling of creatures. A stretch of mental chaos before the sky was white.

29

Within three years of arriving on the island all but four of the Pitcairn men were apparently murdered in a bewildering saga of sex, hatred, drunkenness and revenge. It all started when Faahotu, the Tahitian woman partnered with John Williams, a seaman from Guernsey, died in 1790 from throat cancer. Williams said he wasn't going to live on the island without a woman and attempted forcibly to take one of the three who lived with the six Polynesian men. The Polynesians fought him off. He then tried to leave the island, and to foil him Christian set fire to all the boats.

The following year another woman, Puarei, fell over a cliff while searching for hens' eggs. She'd been partnered with Alexander Smith, who'd changed his name to John Adams. He was the man who'd stood sentry over Bligh with a loaded musket while the 'loyalists' were forced off the *Bounty* into the open boat. He and Williams paired up and seized Vahineatua and Toofaiti from the Polynesian men. Mareva, who was already expected to serve three of the Polynesian men, was then the only woman left to be used by all six of them.

The Polynesian men then resolved to murder all the mutineers except Edward Young, who was marginally kinder to them than the others. They hated these 'whites'. They'd been cheated by them, shanghaied, and beaten if they took yams or a pig. In a coded verse chanted by his partner Mauatua, Christian learned of their plot. He decided to shoot them. Three of the Polynesian men then hid in woodland, taking one of the fought-after women with them. Christian forced the other three to go after them and kill them. They shot two and brought back the third in irons.

The account of these killings seemed like some Old Testament chapter of judgement and nemesis. It scarcely seems credible. It was written up, retrospectively, in the Pitcairn Island Register of Births, Marriages and Remarkable Family Events. The record might have been a decoy. It was half-corroborated, half-contradicted by Teehuteatuaonoa (Jenny), when she eventually returned to Tahiti, and by John Adams.

The given story was that the four remaining Polynesian men: Teimua, Niau, Manarii, and Titahiti, were then treated even more brutally by the mutineers, particularly by McCoy and Quintal. They were beaten and literally had salt rubbed into their wounds.

On 3 October 1793, while the women were in the woods searching for eggs, and the Englishmen were tending the plots of land they'd appropriated for themselves, the Polynesians got hold of guns. They shot John Williams as he was putting up a fence, shot Christian in the back and smashed his head with an axe as he dug his garden, and shot John Mills as he tried to run away. He reached his house, but they broke into it and beat him to death. Teehuteatuaonoa described the carnage:

They now went to Martin's house and shot him: he did not fall immediately, but ran to Brown's house which was not far off. He was there shot a second time. When he fell they beat him on the head with a hammer until he was quite dead. Brown at the same time was knocked on the head with stones and left for dead. As the murderers were going away he rose up and ran. One of them pursued and overtook him. He begged hard for mercy, or that they would not kill him until he had seen his wife. They promised they would spare his life; however one with a musket got behind him and shot him dead.

McCoy was shot at, but escaped and hid in the woods. Quintal heard the shooting and hid there too. Adams was shot through his right shoulder – the bullet came out through his neck. He was then beaten with the butt of the gun and his finger was broken as he covered his face. He ran off and further shots at him missed. Edward Young stayed in his house.

For a week after these murders there were four mutineers, four Polynesian men and eleven women. Young gave his partner Teraura to Teimua and moved into Christian's house with both Faahotu, who'd been with John Williams, and Christian's erstwhile partner Mauatua, who'd just given birth to a daughter Mary.

Manarii then killed Teimua. As revenge the women hounded him into the woods, where Quintal and McCoy, whom he'd tried to kill, were hiding. They throttled him. Young then shot Naiu, and one of the women chopped off Titahiti's head with an axe while he was asleep.

By the end of the third year of colonising Pitcairn the only men left were Young, Adams, McCoy and Quintal. All were mutineers and serial killers. The women and children were then divided among them: four women went to Young, three to Adams, and two each to McCoy and Quintal. Whoever compiled the Pitcairn Register for 1793 kept it brief: 'Massacre of part of the mutineers by the Tahitians. The Tahiti men all killed, partly by jealousies among themselves, the others by the remaining Englishmen. Mary Christian born.'

30

The *Pandora* reached Matavai Bay on 23 March 1791. Tahitians paddled out to the ship and for the desired reward of nails gave Captain Edwards information about the *Bounty* and its crew. Thirteen of its men were still on Tahiti. The master-at-arms Charles Churchill had been murdered by the seaman Matthew Thompson and, as revenge, Churchill's Tahitian friends had then killed Thompson and sacrificed his body to the gods. Fletcher Christian and eight others were long gone with the ship but nobody knew where or, if they did, they weren't saying. Edwards disabused them about Bligh being with Captain Cook on Whytootackee.

Joseph Coleman, the armourer, anxious to show his innocence, swam out to the *Pandora*. He wanted to return to England and be acquitted of any involvement in mutiny. Peter Heywood willingly went out to the ship too. From them Edwards quickly learned the whereabouts of the other wanted men on Tahiti. Some had fled to the mountains and a group had sailed to another part of the island in a thirty-foot schooner called the *Resolution*, beautifully built by the boatswain's mate James Morrison. His resolve had been to sail it to Timor, then sell it to pay for his passage to England. Edwards commandeered it as a tender to the *Pandora*.

All the men were rounded up and treated as pirates. Edwards was indifferent to the pleas of innocence from those who said they'd opposed the mutiny and those who tried to explain that Bligh's boat was so overcrowded they had no option but to remain on board the *Bounty*. As he saw it, it was for an English court to acquit them, or not. He had a supply of chains and handcuffs and the armourer made more. Each prisoner was given a shirt, trousers and a hammock, then manacled, put in leg irons and guarded by the *Pandora* crew with pistols and bayonets. They were told they'd be shot if they spoke to the Tahitians or to each other in Tahitian. The manacles were so tightly locked their wrists and ankles swelled.

Edwards had a structure built on the ship's quarterdeck to contain them. It was round like a funnel and the prisoners called it Pandora's Box. It was eleven feet long and the entrance was through an eighteen-inch-square scuttle at the top, secured by a bolt. There was an iron grate for air. No crew member was to speak to the prisoners except the master-at-arms about their provisions. The heat and stench of the place were intense and it became infested with maggots and vermin.

On 8 May 1791, when all thirteen of the *Bounty* men were locked in this box, Edwards left Tahiti to cruise the Cook, Union, Samoan and Society Islands in search of Fletcher Christian and the rest. At every port of call he circulated Bligh's description of the wanted men.

In violent weather on the evening of 22 June, six weeks after leaving Tahiti, the *Resolution* with nine men on board got separated from the *Pandora* and swept out to sea.

It was armed with blunderbusses and muskets and had netting over the decks to prevent boarding, but its supply of fresh water and provisions was on the *Pandora* waiting to be winched down. Edwards burned false fires and fired guns, but in the storm the men on the schooner could neither see nor hear these. They had two quadrants and two books – *Elements of Navigation* and *Geographical Grammar* – but no charts. They knew they were near the Samoan Islands and they hoped to get to Nomuka and meet up again with the *Pandora*. Within hours they were attacked by Polynesian fishermen in canoes. They shot many of these fishermen dead.

Again a group of men, making their way towards what they hoped might be home, endured the chaos of the ocean, starvation and extremes of thirst and went to the edge of disaster and death. The seemingly straightforward venture of transporting plants from one part of the world to another was lost in time. The chance ramifications of Christian's temper loss fractured yet more lives.

At Tofua, which they mistook for Nomuka, they traded nails for food and water but were again attacked. Tribesmen tried to take their boat. Unsure of where they were, for weeks they sailed round the Friendly and Fijian Islands, then northwest through the Endeavour Strait and the islands of Indonesia. They scavenged food from deserted beaches and were skeletal when they reached the Great Barrier Reef. They didn't know of a passage through it and believed their options to be death by famine or shipwreck. They beat their way over the reef and were saved from starving by the crew of a Dutch vessel who sighted them and gave them food, water and supplies.

After four months they reached the Dutch province of Surabaya on the north coast of Java. They thought they'd reached a safe shore, but the governor didn't believe their story of separation from the *Pandora*. He had Edwards' description of Christian and the missing mutineers from the *Bounty*. The crew of the *Resolution* corresponded in number, spoke only English, were in a hand-hewn boat made from Polynesian wood and couldn't produce any official papers. He concluded they were the wanted men and kept them in prison for a month, then sent them under armed guard to Samarang. But with all such vicissitudes, within the relative framework of what constitutes good luck, those nine men did better than most of the others on the *Pandora*.

For three months Edwards cruised the islands of the South Pacific searching for the *Bounty* and the missing mutineers. He then gave up hope of finding them and headed home. On 29 August 1791 he reached the Great Barrier Reef. He sent a boat to search for a channel through the reef and into the lagoon. The *Pandora* tried to follow through this opening but, in the evening dusk and strong seas, drifted past it and hit the reef.

Within five minutes there was four feet of water in the hold. The men threw guns and everything heavy overboard and pumped and bailed all night, but by dawn water had reached the upper deck and the ship was sinking. There were two canoes and four boats – a launch, an eight-oared pinnace and two six-oared yawls – and there were 134 men on board the *Pandora*. One of the crew tried to lash together the two canoes. He was dashed against the reef. He died and the canoes were lost.

As the ship sank, three of the prisoners – Joseph Coleman the armourer, Charles Norman and Thomas McIntosh both carpenters – were freed from their shackles to work the pumps. The others begged to be unchained and allowed to try to save their lives. Edwards ordered their guards to shoot any who broke free. Men crowded into the boats or flailed in the sea. When the ship lay on its broadside, with the larboard bow completely under water, Edwards passed the prisoners in the box as he made his own escape. Peter Heywood entreated him to have mercy on them. He refused.

But with the ship under water as far as the mainmast and with the box beginning to fill, William Moulter, boatswain's mate on the *Pandora*, drew the bolt on the scuttle. And Joseph Hodges, the armourer's mate, at the risk of his own life unlocked the prisoners' fetters. He said he'd set them free or drown with them.

In seconds the ship went down. Nothing of it was visible but the tip of its mast. The master-at-arms and the sentinels drowned. Peter Heywood was one of the prisoners who survived. He was haunted by memories. 'The cries of the men drowning was at first awful in the extreme but as they sunk and became faint they died away by degrees.'

The boats made for a sandy cay four miles from the disaster. When they returned to the wreck to pick up more men there was silence. Thirty-one of the crew and four of the *Bounty* prisoners had drowned. Naked in the sea Heywood clung to a plank, swam towards the cay and was picked up by one of the boats. James Morrison, builder of the *Resolution,* though still handcuffed, also managed to stay afloat and reach a boat.

The cay was about ninety yards long and sixty wide and without shade. Ninety-nine men reached it. Their only provisions were two casks of water and two bags of bread. Their mouths became so parched they couldn't chew the morsels available. James Connell, a seaman, drank salt water and became delirious with dehydration.

Edwards improvised tents out of sailcloth for himself and those he favoured. The prisoners scorched in the sun. 'We appeared as if dipped in large tubs of boiling water,' Peter Heywood later wrote to his sister Nessy. Their only means of shelter was to bury themselves up to their necks in the burning sand. Heywood asked Edwards if they might make use of an old sail salvaged from the wreck. His request was refused.

After three days the crew and prisoners, in the four boats, headed for Timor and the mercy of the Dutch. They stopped at island shores for oysters and fresh water. At the rocky outcrop Bligh had called Sunday Island, they were attacked by fishermen with bows and arrows. On 2 September, at the north-east point of New Holland, they launched into the Indian Ocean. Ahead of them was a thousand-mile voyage. Their suffering was extreme, 'their temper cross and savage'.

Connell died. The rest reached Timor after eleven ghastly days. 'Nothing could exceed the kindness and hospitality of the governor and other Dutch officers of this settlement, in affording every possible assistance and relief in our distressed condition,' Edwards wrote. For three weeks the men recuperated, then went on a Dutch ship, the *Rembang*, to Samarang, where they were reunited with the crew of the *Resolution*. They all went on to Batavia then home in an English ship, the *Gorgon*.

They arrived at Spithead on 19 June 1792. It was a repeated saga: another ship lost, another court martial, another story of cruelty, heroism, suffering, death, endurance and chaotic departure from the original life plan.

31

Sir Roland remained elusive, though two replies came from London Rookeries. One, asking for a donation, was from a nature reserve with charitable status. The other, from a Mr Stasinopoulos who ran a small hotel in Euston, voiced concern about an elderly guest who called himself Rommel, owed a great deal of money and appeared to have no relatives. Could he be the one we were looking for? My own news was equally discouraging: an automated out-of-the-office reply from Verity and – as ever – alarming news of mother. She'd assaulted one of the residents and caused confusion with the emergency services by her repeated dialling of 999. Firemen had insisted on evacuating the building. There was talk of moving her to a secure psychiatric institution.

I walked to the village square and felt watched by unseen eyes. Bea, the policewoman, was in her garden building a boat, helped by Len, her elderly uncle. They worked with speed and confidence using a handsaw and a hammer and without drawings or reference. I thought of the 'pirates' schooner' the *Resolution*, and how it withstood cruel seas for thousands of miles. I asked questions about the craft of Polynesian boatbuilding and if this boat could reach Mangareva. Bea said it might, if the weather was good.

None of the buildings in the square was locked. There was no theft on the island. The courthouse where the trials were to be held was a simple room with plain tables and chairs and a photograph of Queen Elizabeth the Second on her throne. Pinned on boards outside were public notices to do with the erection of a garden shelter without Council approval and a missing library book, which had a green cover with a computer on it. More urgent notices voiced anxiety and anger about the impending trials:

It has been brought to my attention that some very serious accusations is being sent and passed on from Pitcairn to outsiders concerning people on Pitcairn. This is classed as malicious gossip and like I asked at the public gathering when I made the statement on the same issue, it is a serious offence and that the police can get involved.

If anymore issues are brought to my attention then the police will deal with it immediately. Please let us all try to work together for the good of the island and stop making lives miserable for others.

Thanking you
Steve Christian
Island Mayor

As from 7 June 2004 the Council has passed a resolution that in cases when islanders are involved in personal incidents that could be sensationalised in the media, to refrain from publishing a report of the island until all parties concerned have been consulted. This is in the best interest of all parties concerned and the well being of the island.

Such public trials in this lost and private place seemed harsh – the division of the islanders one against the other, the blame and shame. And there was another missive pinned to the board that would not excite the world's attention. It was from

Dr Thomas H. Scantlebury and dated May 2004. He wrote of his 'undying appreciation to my Pitcairn brother Randy for saving my life and for the cool head which he demonstrated. I will never forget him and will consider him to be a part of me and my family until my dying day.' He thanked Steve too 'for coming into the cave in terrible weather conditions on 11 May at Gudgeon. And no less everlasting appreciation to Jay...'

I asked Rosie about this story. Dr Scantlebury was a Florida doctor who'd served a three-month stint as a Pitcairn locum. One afternoon he went out in a boat with Randy Christian, Steve's son, to take photos of the cliff face and its caves. The sea grew huge, waves whipped up, the boat smashed against the rocks. Both men were big. Scantlebury cracked his head against a rock. Randy dragged him to a secret cave, known to the Pitcairners, beneath the cliff face, at the back of which was dry sand out of reach of the sea. He stemmed the bleeding from the doctor's head. They huddled together for warmth. By evening the islanders feared for them and in treacherous weather Steve and Jay took a boat out to the cave and rescued them.

'Those were acts of heroism,' I said to Rosie. 'Oh it's what we do,' she replied. 'We look out for one another.'

I thought of Joseph Hodges, the armourer's mate on the *Pandora*, who risked his life to unchain prisoners as the ship went down.

After his ordeal Dr Scantlebury became withdrawn. He slept in the clinic and didn't go home to the house assigned to him. He said there was something wrong with its plumbing.

At dawn one wet morning the front door was open and Lady Myre was not in the house. I found her halfway down the Hill of Difficulty, her cyclamen shorts, blue blouson top, pouch bag, face and hands sticky with mud. She seemed to have lost something and was prodding around in thick tyre marks that veered into the ditch.

A woeful saga followed. She'd been bitten to death, not had a wink of sleep and there was no word from Sir Roland. On her way to the jetty in search of a ship she'd met Smiley on his quad bike and he'd said he'd teach her to drive, so she could at least tour the island. She'd accelerated instead of braking, veered off the road, hit her head on a tree and dislodged a gold filling from one of her molars. It was twenty-four-carat. She might have swallowed it but perhaps it was in the mud. Smiley was sweet but she only wanted to be with me.

I made a desultory show of looking for the filling, wiped her hands and knees with half a packet of Wet Ones and walked with her to the health centre. Steve the mayor, engineer, cat castrator, rescuer of Dr Scantlebury and accused rapist, was also the island's dentist.

We waited until the current locum, Les, arrived. He wore shorts, his feet were bare, and he was soon going home to South Island on the *Braveheart*. The dental drill had been donated to the island in 1954. It looked industrial.

Lady Myre refused to open her mouth to have her cavity inspected. She said her pieces of luggage were numbered, the inventory was in her bumbag and in case seven was an emergency dental kit of analgesics and temporary fillings. It would suffice until she reached Tahiti, Panama, Christchurch – any-where.

I wondered why she'd have a dental kit but no mosquito net. Les weighed us both, perhaps because he'd no other help to offer. He didn't know when the drill had last been used. Most of the islanders had false teeth.

Lady Myre and I walked back through groves of banana palms and citrus trees. We explored the neglected remains of Thursday October Christian's house, looked at the *Bounty* can-non and anchor, and the grave of Alexander Smith/John Adams. Such were the museum pieces of the island's murder-ous past. 'Why are you here?' Lady Myre asked and I embarked on my usual spiel about the narrative consequences of random happenings. She began to cry and said she'd never felt more lonely. I told her to come along because there might be enough hot water for a shower, and that Sir Roland might have sent a message. But there wasn't, and he hadn't.

32

On a rock at St Paul, high above the crash of the waves, I pon-dered the history of Pitcairn. I was unconvinced that all the supposed murders had happened, or that within three years only four out of the fifteen men who reached Pitcairn were still alive. The account of this carnage came from three sources: a lost notebook written by Edward Young and quoted from by F.W.Beechey in *Narrative of a Voyage to the Pacific and Beering's Strait* published in 1831; from Teehuteatuaonoa – Jenny – who after thirty-one years on Pitcairn returned to

Tahiti on an American ship, the *Sultan*, and told her story to a Captain Dillon who spoke Tahitian and published it in 1829 in the *United Service Journal and Naval and Military Magazine*; and from the self-named fantasist John Adams, who gave his version to Captain Folger, who chanced on Pitcairn in an American whaling ship the *Topaz* in 1808. Folger stayed about five or six hours on the island. Adams by then was the sole survivor of the mutineers and he was keen to assert his own innocence of murder and worse.

All three accounts blamed the Polynesian men for most of the killings. But the Polynesians were outnumbered by the mutineers and had no guns or ammunition. And there was a lack of forensic evidence: no bones or skulls, no burial places, no telling possessions, none of Bligh's maps or charts, or the gold ducats or Spanish dollars given him by the Admiralty. There was the cannon and the anchor and the ship's Bible, but all the useful things had gone. It was possible that an account of events was fabricated for those who remained on Pitcairn to relay.

In my Moleskine notebook I added to my chronology of significant dates:

1789
28 May. Christian in the *Bounty* anchors at Tubuai in the Austral Islands. Bligh, in the open boat, sights the Great Barrier Reef.
6 June. The *Bounty* returns to Tahiti to abduct women and get provisions.
15 June. Bligh's boat arrives at Coupang in the Dutch East Indies.
16 June. The *Bounty* again leaves Tahiti for Tubuai.
June–September. Christian starts building Fort George. There are battles with the islanders.

12 September. The *Bounty* leaves Tubuai for ever.

22 September. The *Bounty* arrives at Tahiti. Fifteen of the crew opt to stay there.

23 September. The *Bounty* leaves Tahiti for the last time with nine mutineers and eighteen abducted Tahitian girls and young men. September–December. Christian searches for an uninhabited island to colonise.

1790

15 January. Fletcher Christian arrives at Pitcairn Island in the *Bounty*.

23 January. The *Bounty* is burned.

14 March. Bligh reaches Portsmouth after his ordeal in an open boat.

22 October. Bligh court-martialled for the loss of the *Bounty* but acquitted of wrongdoing.
November. The *Pandora* leaves Britain captained by Edward Edwards to round up all the mutineers.

1791

23 March. The *Pandora* reaches Tahiti. The *Bounty* crew there are rounded up and put in irons.

8 May. The *Pandora* leaves Tahiti.

3 August. Bligh leaves England in the *Providence* on a second bread-fruit mission.

28 August. The *Pandora* wrecked on the Great Barrier Reef. Four of the *Bounty* prisoners die.

The lives of the Pitcairn fugitives were gone with faint trace. Those who recorded their fate used the bleached tone of the chronicler: 'Arrived in 1790. Died in ... Shot in the back as he tended his yams' ... 'Murdered in the mountains ...' But the focus of those restless seafaring men would not have been to settle as peasant farmers. The island was not a place for those who'd known wider shores.

It was my hunch that Christian and some of the murderers had left the island. Fear of reprisal would have diminished with time. There was enough expertise among them to build an equivalent ship to James Morrison's schooner. It took him less than a year. The women could make sails, the Polynesian men knew the qualities of wood and how to hew it, the English had the ship's forge. Those who got away would have sworn to silence the women they left behind.

I observed the ocean and listened to its rhythmic chords. Two spouting whales played. They rolled to the surface then dived. Perhaps the men left in good weather in small boats like the one Bea was making with such ease, or as itinerant crew on a passing whaler. Americans hunted whales in these waters. The Pitcairn Register recorded the arrival of an unnamed ship on 27 December 1795. Adams spoke to Captain Folger of three ships that had called and how one sent a boat to the shore. It was feasible to work a passage back to England from China or America.

There were rumours that Christian made frequent visits to an aunt in Cumberland in the 1800s. And in 1808 Peter Heywood was sure he saw him in Fore Street near the docks in Plymouth. He walked fast to catch up with him. The man turned. Heywood was emphatic it was Christian. The man then ran because he'd been recognised. Heywood chased him but didn't catch him. He wondered whether to make more enquiries but feared all the trouble and pain this might lead to, so did nothing. He recounted this to the explorer Sir John Barrow, who wrote a history of the mutiny in 1831.

Children born on Pitcairn in the 1790s would not have been spared the sight of the murder of their fathers and the abuse of their mothers. Nor could they have been certain of their parentage. Four men were left on the island by 1793. The eleven women were expected to serve them in every way.

A year after the alleged massacre the Register recorded 'a great desire in many of the women to leave the island'. They built themselves a boat to escape. Perhaps they'd learned how to do this from the men. Teehuteatuaonoa even tore down her house for its planks and nails. This boat was launched on 15 August 1794 and, Young said, 'according to our expectations she upset'. He called them 'a few ignorant women drifting upon the waves'.

Prisoners of the island and trapped in a rapacious place, the women grouped together to avoid the men. They lived separately from them and conspired to murder them as they slept. The hatred was mutual. The men, now far outnumbered by the women, became afraid of them. Quintal said he wouldn't 'laugh, joke or give anything to the girls'. In his journal Young wrote

It was agreed among us that the first female who misbehaved should be put to death and this punishment was to be repeated until we could discover the real intentions of the women...

The women formed a party whenever their displeasure was excited and hid themselves in the unfrequented parts of the island carefully providing themselves with firearms. In this manner the men were kept in continual suspense, dreading the result of each disturbance.

Into this lawless environment where violence, sex and incest were allied, babies were born. All the children had British names: Sarah McCoy, Jane and Arthur Quintal, Dinah and Rachel Adams, Polly, Robert, George, William, Edward, Dolly and James Young.

In April 1798 McCoy, who'd once worked in a Scottish distillery, turned the *Bounty*'s copper kettle into a still and made a fiendish liquor from the Te-root (*Cordyline terminalis*). From that date he and Quintal were alcoholic. When Teatuahitea, or Sarah as she was called, caught too few fish, Quintal bit off her ear. McCoy became entirely disreputable and had frequent alcohol-induced fits. The Pitcairn Register recorded that in one of these he 'fastened a stone to his neck threw himself from the rocks into the sea and was drowned'. More likely he was despatched, for he was found by a child, in a rock pool, with his hands and feet bound.

The women and their children built houses and fences, cultivated crops, made canoes for fishing, trapped pigs and birds, cooked, sewed and survived. They spoke a patois and they mapped and named their island: McCoy's Drop, Where Freddie Fall, Break Im Hip, Nellie Fall, Dan Fall, Down the Hole, Headache and, more cheerfully, Bang Iron Valley, Up the Beans, Lucky Valley and Johncatch'acow.

In 1799 Quintal's partner, the unfortunate one-eared Teatuahitea, fell over a cliff while collecting birds' eggs. She left four children, all perhaps fathered by him. Despite there being nine women and only three men, Adams maintained Quintal then forcibly tried to take Teraura, who was living with Young, and Teehuteatuaonoa, who'd been claimed by Adams. Adams and Young retaliated by killing him:

One day when he was in John Adams' house Quintal was set upon and overpowered by the two other men. By means of a hatchet the dreadful work of death was soon completed. The daughter of John Mills (who lived to the age of 93) then a young girl of eight or nine years of age was an eyewitness of the awful deed and used to relate how terrified were all of the little band of women and children who beheld the blood-bespattered walls.

Fifteen young men landed on Pitcairn in 1790. Nine years later thirteen of them had apparently been murdered. Twenty children were left on the island: nine boys and eleven girls. It was the only place they knew.

Edward Young died of asthma on Christmas Day 1800. John Adams was left in terrible command. In a notebook he began his autobiography, but didn't get far: 'I was born at Stanford Hill in the parrish of St Jon Hackney Middlesex of poor But honast parrents. My farther Was Drouned in the Theames thearfore he left Me and 3 More poore Orfing' – thus the founding father of Pitcairn, the one who definitely didn't leave and wasn't murdered, the only mutineer still there in 1808 when Captain Folger arrived in the *Topaz*.

He became a self-appointed chief, the inheritor of a kingdom. He ruled nine women and a host of fatherless children. After a drunken fit he had some sort of vision in which God told him to show the way forward to his people. With his interpretation of the *Bounty* Bible, he ruled them all. The children grew up brainwashed by him and in service to him. Advised by the angel Gabriel, he enforced morning, afternoon and evening prayers and ruled that everyone must fast on Wednesdays and Fridays. Working women fainted as they hoed and slaved. Their Polynesian identity was taken from them and they were severed from their rich Tahitian roots. They chanted from the Bible and had no verbal humour or irony. As the island's children grew up, they married cousins, half-brothers, uncles, aunts. Adams officiated, using the island's single wedding ring. These children inherited strong limbs, diabetes, asthma, and a lack of candour.

Adams ordered that his daughter Dinah be shot when she had an illegitimate child by Matthew Quintal's grandson Edward. Her sin was fornication. When no one would shoot her, Adams attempted it himself. Edward's father, Arthur, restrained him. Perhaps Dinah didn't know that her father had murdered Arthur's father by cracking his head with an axe. Perhaps Edward knew and sought revenge.

I wandered back to Adamstown in dappled light. Bea was painting her boat yellow. She'd called it the *Dolphin*. She said an announcement had been made over the intercom asking if anyone had seen me and knew where I was. I wondered if this was concern for my safety or suspicion as to what I might be doing.

33

Lady Myre and I were invited to supper by the governor's representative Wayne and his Albanian wife Tania. He was young but old, and with the demeanour of a secret agent. He'd been posted to Pitcairn for a year to deal with the logistics of the trials, then he'd be transferred to some other uncommercial outpost of the old colonial world.

The house assigned to him was clean and well-equipped, as neatly built as the prison and with all amenities. It had a private generator and an electrically operated mosquito repellent. There were shelves of CDs, DVDs, and videos. There was a lone cat, neutered by a government vet and with a flea collar. All that the officials might want was shipped with them and extra supplies were brought on Nigel Jolly's *Braveheart*. They kept to a standard, mixed with each other and seemed no part of Pitcairn. The islanders called them visitors and seldom remembered them when they left.

Equally polished and pristine was the other guest, Mary the schoolteacher, plump and complacent, in a well-ironed white blouse, her white hair washed in good shampoo. She too occupied a government house, but a new, smarter schoolhouse was being built for her use. She too was on the island for a year. She was about seventy and had gone to New Zealand from Hampstead. Her husband, who wasn't with her, was a painter. In her school were four children, aged four to fourteen. She said she had one rule: 'Keep your hands and feet to yourself.'

The food had an Albanian slant: spicy chicken and rice, salads, barbecued fish. There was a chilled New Zealand Chardonnay, and an elaborately decorated chocolate cake.

I foolishly asked, 'Where did you get that?' 'From the French patisserie down at the bay,' Mary said, then spurted with laughter.

Lady Myre was wonderfully herself in a rustling green skirt and a pink feathery boa. She'd painted each of her toenails a different colour. 'Don't you love them?' she asked Wayne. 'Aren't they jewels?'

We ate on a verandah overlooking the sea. The talk was of planned improvements for the island: the reconstruction of the jetty, shipping links with French Polynesia, the feasibility of an airstrip, a concrete surface for the Hill of Difficulty – though it was thought that if mud stuck to the wheels of quad bikes from tracks to the houses and gardens, they'd skid off the concrete and into the sea. All the grant allocation had to be spent by the end of the financial year, but not much had yet been agreed.

I asked a few questions about the forthcoming trials.

'The truth is going to come out,' Wayne said.

A notice had been issued requiring all islanders to hand in their guns before the court convened. One or two had refused. The guns were to be taken from them out of fear of 'hot-headedness' or that they might be used against defendants or victims.

Conversation shifted to Lady Myre and her iPod, the temporary dressing on her tooth, her attempt to learn to drive a quad bike.

'Are you travelling together?' Wayne asked.

She said we were, I said we weren't. There was a thoughtful quiet. Then she went into a performance about her time on the Shaw Savill Line and how she'd starred in Kenya as Winnie in Samuel Beckett's *Happy Days* and the audience had left in droves at the interval. 'Is it me you're after, Willie?' she declaimed, 'or is it something else? Is it a kiss you're after, Willie? or is it something else?'

No one knew what she was talking about. They looked uncomfortable, even alarmed. 'And you,' Mary asked of me, 'what's your career?' I talked of the flightless rail and the mutiny on the *Bounty* and how I'd spent three months on

Juan Fernandez, off the coast of Chile, because of my interest in Alexander Selkirk, who'd been marooned there for four years – and did she know he was the prototype for Robinson Crusoe?

It seemed there was no transparency from anyone except Lady Myre, who perhaps was entirely mendacious but gave the impression of being frank. The paranoia and concealment of Pitcairn's history pervaded the room. Mary then said Wednesday at her school was Culture Day, and Lady Myre and I were invited to attend this week, as special guests. Nola Young would be teaching the children how to cook the manioc root and there'd be one or two other subjects of discussion. We should be there at ten.

Lady Myre wanted to get back to the computer while the generator was still working. 'Come along,' she said to me as if I were her spouse or dog. She asked if she might take the remains of her supper with her to feed the cats. She said she was a bird person really, but life was life, and she loved it. I suspected more candid conversation might begin after we'd gone.

The moon was high and clear and seemed further away than at home. Lady Myre linked my arm as we passed the unfinished prison and the health clinic where Dr Scantlebury had slept at night. At our lodging, at either side of the door to the outside lavatory – the dunny as it was called – stood two large land crabs. Each had the legs of a cockroach sticking from its mouth. I shared this observation with Lady Myre, who made a trilling noise of alarm. There was no communication from Sir

Roland or from Verity. There was, though, a familiar update on mother, who'd thrown her bedding out of the window at Sunset View.

34

In August 1791, on a ship called *Providence* with an escort brig the *Assistant*, Bligh left on a second attempt to take breadfruit from Tahiti to the West Indies. Two botanists were on board to supervise the venture and to collect rare plant specimens for the Royal Botanical Gardens at Kew.

It took thirty-six weeks to reach Tahiti and for the first six of those Bligh was very ill. He thought he was going to die and he assigned command to his lieutenants. He had a constant and terrible headache and 'burning heat' in his skin, his face was flushed, he lost his balance, found the least sound intolerable, had a sinking feeling in his stomach, 'a lowness and flurry of spirits' and couldn't bear the sun on him. The surgeon thought he had some nervous illness.

The *Providence* passed Pitcairn in April 1792. Like Edwards in the *Pandora* the previous year, Bligh had no inkling of what was going on there. He again warned his crew they mustn't say anything to the Tahitians about Captain Cook's death, or why all these breadfruit were wanted, and he threatened 'disgrace and punishment' to anyone who disobeyed his commands.

The Tahitian chiefs were again flattered that he'd come to see them as King George the Third's emissary. Their queen Obereroah visited him on the ship, but was so corpulent she had to be winched on board in a chair. She asked for beads and other things. Bligh declined her reciprocal offer of one of her maidservants.

There was the usual barter. The English wanted exotic souvenirs: war mats and wickerwork breastplates adorned with sharks' teeth. The Tahitians wanted nails, firearms, hatchets, knives, scissors, mirrors, brandy. But they were ever more wary of these English mariners. The crew of the *Pandora* had brought an infectious epidemic and given them more venereal disease. The Tahitians told Bligh of the now fatherless sons and daughters of the mutineers. 'I have seen none of the sons and some are said to be dead,' Bligh wrote in his log. He did, though, see the midshipman George Stewart's daughter 'a fine child, a very pretty creature'. Her father had drowned, aged twenty-three, in the wreck of the *Pandora*.

From the chiefs Bligh learned of Christian's return to Tahiti, his attempt to settle on Tubuai, his second visit, then departure for some unknown place. He heard how the men who'd stayed built the *Resolution,* which was taken by Captain Edwards, and how Churchill and Thompson became jealous of each other, so Churchill stole Thompson's musket and shot him dead and then friends of Thompson beat Churchill's brains out. The chiefs told Bligh that though they'd given Christian sails and all he wanted, they'd treated him with coldness and were happy when Edwards carried the rest of the English away.

As in 1788, Bligh set up a nursery on shore for the plants to establish. He intended to sail 'with every inch of space filled up with plants' and by 6 May 1792 he had 1281 vigorous saplings potted. A greenhouse was created on the quarterdeck, the sailmakers made covers and the carpenters made scuttles to give air when the portholes couldn't be opened. The ship was cleaned and painted, a hundred tons of water were casked from the River Matavai, hogs and fowls were caged on board, the islanders helped load the breadfruit and the ship sailed in August. Two Tahitian boys were on board. One had stowed away and when found became known as Jacket, or Bobbo. The other, Maititi, sailed as a servant to Bligh.

Bligh's second breadfruit voyage was relatively uneventful. His route from Tahiti was to Timor through the Torres Strait, across the Indian Ocean, around the Cape, and north-west to Jamaica. On the journey one of the crew died from arrow wounds in a skirmish with fishermen, another from cold and 'an improper use of arrack', and two from malaria contracted in Coupang. The stowaway, Bobbo, was left in Jamaica to help the gardener there, but he died after a few weeks. Nine hundred and twenty-seven of the plants survived. The West Indians hated the taste of breadfruit, though it became an integral part of their diet because no alternative staple food was available.

It took Bligh a year to get back to England after leaving Tahiti. He was elected a Fellow of the Royal Society and given their gold medal for distinguished services to botany and navigation. More generally, he was known as Bounty Bastard Bligh. To his chagrin his account of this second voyage was not wanted. The Admiralty told him, 'At present books of voyages sell so slowly that they do not defray the expence of publishing.'

His Tahitian servant, Maititi, died soon after reaching England and was buried in St Paul's churchyard in Deptford.

35

While Bligh was at sea, the court martial of the accused men
who survived the wreck of the *Pandora* was held in the captain's cabin of HMS *Duke*, anchored at Spithead. It lasted
from 12 to 18 September 1792. Presiding over the process was
Lord Hood, First Lord of the Admiralty. He and eleven captains were to judge which of the accused should live and
which should die.

The defendants were Peter Heywood midshipman, James
Morrison boatswain's mate, Charles Norman carpenter's
mate, Joseph Coleman armourer, Thomas McIntosh carpenter, Thomas Burkett, Thomas Ellison and John Millward seamen, William Muspratt the cook's assistant and Michael
Byrne the violinist. All were charged with the capital offence
of mutiny.

Without Bligh, the Crown was missing its chief witness for
the prosecution, but he'd given an emphatic account at his
own court martial two years previously. He testified that Coleman, Norman and McIntosh had wanted to leave in the boat
with him and had been detained on the *Bounty* by force. He
scathingly indicted Peter Heywood and deemed him as guilty
of mutiny as Christian. The six other men he left to defend
themselves as best they could.

The fracas of the mutiny had happened three and a half
years previously in minutes of confusion and fear. No one

seemed clear of its essential cause, nor was this dwelled on. Many of the prisoners were illiterate. All had endured hardship. They were at the mercy of the recollections of their witnesses – the men who'd survived the open boat journey with Bligh. Only Peter Heywood had the benefit of legal guidance.

Witnesses were called singly to testify. They appeared according to rank – warrant officers then midshipmen. From their recall, a picture of that distant morning emerged: of swearing against Bligh – 'Damn his eyes', 'Shoot the bugger', 'The boat's too good for him'; of Christian lamenting that he'd been in hell; of Bligh without his trousers, his hands tied behind him; of a scramble to get things for survival – water, food and clothes.

There were confused accounts of who'd been armed and who hadn't, but Thomas Ellison and Thomas Burkett were both found guilty of being armed with muskets while aiding Fletcher Christian to take the ship. Ellison was fifteen when he'd signed up with the *Bounty* as an able seaman. He was living in Deptford at the time, needed employment, and the ship was there. He was five feet three, with dark hair and had his name and 25 October 1788 – the date he'd arrived in Tahiti – tattooed on his right arm. The charge against him was that, at Christian's bidding, he left the helm of the *Bounty*, picked up a cutlass, ran towards Bligh and called, 'Damn him, I'll be sentinel over him.' To the court he said:

I hope your honour will take my inexperienced youth into consideration as I never did or meant any harm to anyone, much more to my Commander to whose care I was recommended. He took great pains with me and spoke to Mr Samuel his clerk to teach me writing and arithmetic, and I believe would have taught me further had not this happened. I must have been very ungrateful if I had in any respect assisted in this unhappy affair against my Commander and benefactor, so I hope honorable gentlemen you'll be so kind as to take my case into consideration, as I was no more than between sixteen and seventeen years of age when this was done.

Burkett was five feet nine with brown hair, many tattoos and a face pitted with smallpox scars. He could read and write and he'd left a son on Tahiti. It was testified that he held a knife over Bligh and helped drag him from his cabin.

John Millward was also indicted for being armed, though evidence against him was confused. He was twenty-two at the time of the mutiny, five feet five, 'very much Tatowed in Different parts' and the son of an illiterate sailor. To the judges he said he'd only taken hold of a cutlass and pistols because he was afraid to disobey Christian's orders. He'd thought Fryer intended to retake the ship. He'd thrown his jacket into the loyalists' boat for his messmate George Simpson, 'with my prayers for their protection'. He said he didn't know how he could have acted differently.

James Morrison's defence was that Bligh begged him not to get into the boat, because it was so overloaded. He said he'd handed down cutlasses, pork and gourds of water, and Bligh had shaken his hand and promised he'd do him justice in England. John Fryer, the master, praised him as a steady, sober, attentive man and denied he was armed, but another witness swore he saw him with a cutlass. 'Amidst such *Crowd*, *Tumult* and *Confusion* might not the Arms in the hands of another wedged by my side *easily* be thought to be in *my possession?*' Morrison asked the court. A third witness said that as the boat was veered astern Morrison had called out, 'If my friends inquire after me, tell them I am somewhere in the South Seas.'

With William Muspratt, too, there was uncertain evidence as to whether he was armed. Two witnesses said he was. And he'd deserted while on Tahiti. He was tattooed, had a scarred chin and a black beard. His father had hung himself from an apple tree the year before the *Bounty* sailed and an inquest had ruled the cause to be lunacy. Muspratt, like Morrison, claimed Bligh asked him not to get into the overcrowded boat. He tried to discredit all the evidence as too contradictory to be reliable, and said it was a great misfortune no one had tried to rescue the ship. 'It might have been done,' he claimed. 'Thompson was the only Centinel upon the Arms Chest.'

Michael Byrne pleaded that he was almost blind and that he'd wanted to leave with Bligh but Churchill had threatened to lock him up if he did. And Christian had said, 'We must not part with our fiddler.'

Much of the trial centred on midshipman Peter Heywood. A whole day was accorded to his cross-examination. He had the advantage of being educated and articulate with influential friends. Not for the last time the law favoured the well-to-do. His lawyer, Aaron Graham, wasn't averse to paying witnesses to give the desired evidence. Lord Howe, First Lord of the Admiralty, was a friend both of Heywood's family and of one of the judges. Bligh, his most emphatic detractor, was at sea.

The charges against him were that he helped hoist

the launch, was armed with a cutlass and, when asked by Bligh to accompany him, laughed and remained in the ship. In mitigation, Purcell the carpenter said he saw him drop the cutlass and go below and that he seemed confused by what was going on.

Heywood swore before the court and the 'tribunal of Almighty God' that he was innocent. He said he was sleeping in his hammock and hadn't the slightest intimation of what was going on. His 'faculties were benumbed' when he saw Bligh bound and pushed into a boat. He helped haul out the launch in order to assist Bligh, not Christian. He put provisions into it and 'in doing this it was that my hand touched the cutlass', his intention was innocent, he was in a state of stupor. His extreme youth and inexperience influenced his conduct. He thought that to go in the boat would mean 'inevitable destruction'. He thought he'd be starved to death or drowned. He was at the time only sixteen, there was no one to advise him, he was ignorant of naval discipline, he hadn't known he was committing a crime.

He admitted he put saving his own life above other considerations but he'd never have betrayed Bligh. Only a 'monster of depravity' would have done that. He went below because he didn't want to be identified with the mutineers... He hadn't wanted to go to Tubuai, but Christian forced him in case he gave intelligence information when a ship arrived. He'd welcomed the arrival of the *Pandora* and had immediately given himself up. 'Before God,' he said, he was 'innocent of plotting abetting or assisting either by word or deed in the taking of the ship', All witnesses said he was of good and amiable character, and that when the *Pandora* arrived on Tahiti he offered himself up voluntarily and gave all information on the whereabouts of the mutineers.

Accounts of the mutineers' trial in the daily papers were eclipsed by breaking news from France of the massacre of aristocrats and royalists. On 18 September the court acquitted Charles Norman, Joseph Coleman, Thomas McIntosh and Michael Byrne. All were released immediately. Charges were declared proven against Peter Heywood, James Morrison, Thomas Ellison, Thomas Burkett, John Millward and William Muspratt. They were condemned to die by being hanged by the neck on board a naval ship of war. The court gave the right to appeal for the king's pardon to Heywood, Morrison and Muspratt.

'We are in an Agony of Suspense – I can scarcely support my own misery, much less keep up poor Mama's dejected spirits,' Nessy, Heywood's sister, wrote. Aaron Graham was quick to reassure them both. The king's Attorney General, who'd attended the trial, told him that his friend Peter was 'as safe as if he had not been condemned'.

Two days later, on 27 October 1792, Heywood and Morrison were read the king's pardon and recommended to atone for their evil conduct by future good behaviour. Heywood read a statement of gratitude for his sovereign's mercy and gave an assurance that his future life would be faithfully devoted to his service. Morrison's response was not recorded.

On the morning of 29 October, a Monday, a crowd gathered in Portsmouth Harbour. At eleven o'clock Thomas Ellison,

John Millward and Thomas Burkett were taken to the fo'c'sle of the ship *Brunswick*. Bags were put over their heads and nooses round their necks. At eleven twenty-six a gun was fired. 'Thomas Burkett was Run up to the Starboard Fore Yard Arm, Millward and Ellison to the Larboard and There Hung Agreeable to their Sentence.'

Muspratt didn't receive his pardon until 11 February 1793. The stress of waiting and the execution of his three friends so shocked him that in those interim four months he couldn't speak to anyone 'nor by any means be prevailed on to do so'.

In 1794 Edward Christian, who was a lawyer, published the minutes of the court martial with an appendix giving a spirited defence of his youngest brother, Fletcher. Bligh gave a reasoned and bitter response, but he did not come out of the affair well and a taint attached to him of sadism and overly harsh command.

Peter Heywood accepted an invitation from the presiding judge at his trial, Lord Hood, to sail with him on the *Victory* as his midshipman, and he was promoted to the rank of lieutenant. Lord Hood was a friend of his uncle.

36

The rain set in. I lost count of the days and time took on a strange dimension. Lady Myre surfed the net or lay on my bed working her way through a thousand tunes and drinking exotic cocktails of her own devising. I felt I'd been on the island for ever. When I could get a look in on the computer I logged on to CNN news. I learned of car-bombings in Iraq, massacre in Burundi, the blowing-up of a bus in Israel, the banning of same-sex marriages in Missouri. *The Scream* was stolen from the Munch Museum in Oslo. At other times I sat in Christian's cave in my waterproofs and made notes about significant happenings consequent on Christian's theft of a coconut:

1792
18 June. Survivors from the *Pandora* arrive at Spithead.
12 September. Court martial of the ten crewmen who stayed with Fletcher Christian on the *Bounty*.
29 October. Thomas Ellison, Thomas Burkett and John Millward are hung at Spithead.

1793
27 January. Bligh arrives at the West Indies with the breadfruit.
 3 September. The *Providence* arrives back in Britain.
20 September. Christian and four other mutineers murdered on Pitcairn.
 4 October. All the remaining Polynesian men murdered on Pitcairn.

Often I'd chat with Rosie in her kitchen. We'd cut bananas lengthwise, she'd put them in a drying machine, then we'd pack them in little polythene packets. The process was sticky, and a cloud of fruit flies hovered. She'd talk of the Resurrection and the prospect of the arrival of the Messiah. She said when He came the good would have eternal life and sinners would be damned. Only if they repented, admitted their sins and clung to the cross could they be saved.

Sixteen public toilets had been erected on the island, all in places of natural beauty. They were white, cupboard-like structures, with flushes, water tanks and taps. One afternoon as I passed one of them Lady Myre dashed out, her turquoise shorts round her knees. She was batting at herself and quacking. Her lips had gone blue and I feared she was going to die. Wasps swirled round her. She'd opened the cover of a hymnal, which she supposed had been left for its paper, and there was a nest of them in it. One stung her on her hand, another on her bottom. In my body belt I had antihistamine cream and I tended to her as best I could.

'You're my saviour,' she grizzled. 'I want to go home.'

Her mishaps were frequent. On the day she dug for hours in Bang Iron Valley with a garden trowel, hoping to find the *Bounty*'s gold ducats, she lost the Cartier watch Sir Roland had given her on their twenty-fifth wedding anniversary. We searched among ferns and gunnera, twisted branches and tangled weeds, but couldn't find it. When we picnicked at St Paul's Point her panama hat blew over the cliff and floated on the waves like a signal of distress. When she fished in Bounty Bay she fell into the sea. She dangled a baited hook at the end of a piece of wire in the water and within seconds snared a large nanwee. Inspired by such quick success, she again straggled the wire in the bay. Jackie the frigate bird flew off with the caught fish. Lady Myre turned and exclaimed, the wire caught round a bollard and tightened and she didn't let go of it. I wondered at her smile as she clambered to the shore.

Her searches for her husband and passage off the island were always unrewarding. Replies from shipping companies and the Pitcairn Commissioner's Office in Auckland were consistent. No ships were scheduled to stop at Pitcairn. If anything came up she'd be notified. Disappointment made her wilt. At a time of intense depression she wore the same outfit for an entire day. Her horror of cockroaches meant she seldom used the bathroom. She abluted with Wet Ones, colognes and lotions. Each night she slept under my mosquito net and I in her room with her luggage. Often she'd wake me to say someone was watching her through the window or that a creature was rustling under the bed or to ask if she could come in with me for a cuddle.

Rosie cracked coconuts in half with one blow from her machete, grated the flesh and mixed it with green bananas. She chopped sweet potato and butternut squash and stewed leftover roast lamb and wild beans.

Over the intercom came a public announcement from the shop: bread, ham, bacon, frozen pastry and chicken pieces had been priced and entered into the day books. Each household had a book in which all purchases were recorded. No individual was allowed more than six of anything. Every few months the books were collected for auditing. I remarked that I thought Adventism forbade the eating of pig. Rosie spoke of the decline of standards: smoking, drinking, trading on the Sabbath. 'But we still look out for each other,' she said again. They exchanged oranges for coconuts, pawpaws for vegetables, fish for bread and cake, they saved each other's lives and the lives of strangers. They interdepended.

She rued the suspicion and animosity that publicity for the trials aroused, the division between families, the depression of mothers at the violation of their daughters. She longed for it all to be finished and for the spotlight of interest to be turned elsewhere. The crimes of which the island's men were now accused had happened twenty years previously. She favoured a truth-and-reconciliation process, a learning of respect for women. She said you couldn't be a girl on Pitcairn and not have sex. It seemed it all went back to Fletcher Christian and those barefoot pirates with cutlasses and tattoos.

Rosie was wistful about joining her daughters in New Zealand and seeing her grandchildren. But Hank loved his island, its traditions and memories, where the sun rose, the church, the longboats and the cliffs. For him it was where God lived and spoke.

She talked of the island's more recent history – how in 1856, when there was a population of 194, it was overcrowded, so the British government sent a transport ship and moved them all to Norfolk Island, an abandoned penal colony ten times the size of Pitcairn, 3500 miles west, and close to New Zealand. Most adapted and preferred it, but some yearned to go home, the way some people do, however hard home might be. Sixteen returned, drawn to the life they knew.

I thought how the gene pool needed mixing. How they'd all intermarried for far too long and that it was a worn-out island, its earth eroded, its native trees felled.

Rosie didn't mention the names of the men on the island accused of sex crimes, but details were on the internet. Investigations began after a Kent policewoman, Gail Cox, went to Pitcairn in 1999 to train an islander in community policing. She gave the Pitcairn girls leaflets about sexual harassment. One of them then told her how Randy Christian, the man who saved Dr Scantlebury's life, had used her for sex for a decade from when she was a young girl. Many allegations of sex abuse followed: twenty-one accusations of rape, forty-one of indecent assault, two of gross indecency with a girl under fourteen. British police investigated. They called it Operation Unique.

A picture emerged of men who, when the chance was there, preyed on girls, like they caught fish when they went to the shore: of rape in bushland or in a boat in Bounty Bay; of a girl accosted when sent to collect firewood; of a schoolgirl groped when she came out of a public toilet; of a ten-year-old molested as she played tag. It seemed that sex wasn't much different from abuse by the mutineers of the Polynesian girls they'd abducted. One plaintiff said she'd tried to object to rape but there was no point. 'I just lay there and let him get it over and done with. The quicker he did it the quicker I was able to go.'

Steve Christian, the mayor, was charged with five rapes including that of a twelve-year-old girl. One victim said, 'He seemed to take it on himself to initiate all the girls and it was like we were his harem.' His son Randall, chairman of the Internal Committee of the Island Council, was accused of four rapes and five indecent assaults. Len Brown, Steve Christian's father-in-law – the quiet man helping Bea build her boat – was charged with two rapes in a watermelon patch. His son Dave Brown was charged with nine indecent assaults including molesting a fifteen-year-old girl on a spear-fishing trip. It was all, he said, 'a normal part of Pitcairn life. It didn't seem wrong.' The postmaster Dennis Christian faced two charges of sexual assault and one of indecent assault against young girls. Terry Young, a descendant of midshipman Edward Young, was charged with one rape and six indecent assaults.

I wondered about unwanted sex in small closed communities and the breaking of silence, so necessary and terrible. Girls didn't talk about it because what was the point? They were treated the same as their mothers and great-great-great-grandmothers before them. The abusers felt they themselves were now abused by a distant colonial power. Some of the island's men accused British police of pressurising the women to lay charges. Steve Christian's wife Olive, mother of Randy, daughter of Len, said sex on the island was a Polynesian tradition: 'We all thought sex was like food on the table.'

The defence for the accused was that the age of consent in Polynesia was lower than in Britain and that Pitcairners had renounced British citizenship when they burned the *Bounty*, an act they ritually celebrated by setting fire to an effigy of it every January. From then on, they said, Pitcairners ceased to be under British protection or accountable to British law. It was claimed that Britain had never taken formal possession of Pitcairn or officially informed the islanders that British legislation such as the Sexual Offences Act of 1956 was applicable to them. Pitcairn had no trained police, lawyers or appeal structure. Its own ordinances were to do with property and land use. And now Pitcairn crime was to be tried by New Zealand lawyers, under English law. Bewilderment was real. The alleged offences went back so far, the defendants were accused of breaking laws they said they didn't know existed. 'No one shall be held guilty of any criminal offence on account of any act or omission which did not constitute a criminal offence at the time it was committed' was a clause of the Human Rights Act of 1998 according to British law. Did that statute apply to Pitcairn? From the girls' point of view sex was violent and unwanted and they had no knowledge of their rights.

There had been previous convictions on the island in the 1970s for 'carnal knowledge of minors', rape and the abuse of girls. Men had served three-month terms in the old prison, which now housed farm machinery, and had then gone free. No reform of the sexual culture of the island followed those sentences. A couple of wardens had been sent from New Zealand to guard the prisoners, give them meals and release them to work the longboats.

Rosie blamed the bringing in of illicit alcohol by outsiders and the demise of religion, which she thought had led to a culture of wrongdoing by most of the men of a certain age. Hank didn't want to talk about any of it. He disliked the divisiveness of it all.

The defence lawyers had encouraged the men to plead not guilty and to expect to be freed on legal technicalities and receive compensation. A bill passed by the British parliament in 2002 allowed the trials to take place in New Zealand, which would have been more expedient and less costly. But two years later the accused won a legal right to be tried on Pitcairn. So a prison had to be built, in case charges were upheld, and satellite communication links were installed. Three judges, prosecution and defence lawyers, court staff and journalists were to travel to the island, doubling the number of people there. Witnesses abroad would give evidence by video.

Rosie didn't see how there could be a good outcome for the islanders. If the defence won on the grounds that Pitcairners weren't answerable to British law, where would their subsidy and support then come from? They lacked the expertise or resources for self-government. They made no real money from selling stamps and coins, T-shirts, macramé baskets, fish and dried bananas. And if they weren't answerable to British law, was Pitcairn a zone of immunity from any crime? What code should they live by, when instinct and ancestral law had got them into this trouble? If the accused men pleaded guilty, they'd serve some kind of sentence, it would all be over and wouldn't attract the curiosity of the wider world. Pitcairn society wouldn't be so damaged. Again she talked of the need for restorative justice to heal wounds, teach new attitudes and help victims and offenders create a safe community. But the United Kingdom and New Zealand governments thought that without a full police process it would seem as if the offences were being overlooked. Abuse was endemic. The crimes were grave and violent and the victims were children.

It seemed a beleaguered place. It rained and rained. Many times, because of cyclones, storms and the howling wind, the longboats couldn't brave the sea or reach the shore. The previous year four government officials had tried to visit to assess the needs of the islanders. They travelled via Mangareva in Graham Wragg's catamaran. For four nights the sea was too rough to approach the makeshift jetty and they rode the waves. A longboat then went out for them. They transferred to it, but after an hour's respite the wind again picked up, the waves raged, the boat couldn't safely approach the shore and they spent a night in the open boat in torrential rain. At daylight it went to the lee of the island, to the rocks at west harbour where there was no jetty or mooring place. The officials waded ashore exhausted, bedraggled and freezing, their clothes and belongings soaked, then clambered half a mile along the rocks and got on the back of muddy quad bikes in pouring rain.

Rosie thought the experience might help focus their minds to the fact that if Pitcairners were to survive with any quality of life they must have a proper jetty and investment in their island.

Nola Young came to collect Lady Myre and me at ten in the morning for Culture Day at the school. It was to be about the virtues of the indigenous manioc root. She was a small, preoccupied woman and she carried a basket of dark-brown crinkly roots. The lanes were slippery from the rain. As we walked, she told us the day would come when no one would visit the island and no one would leave it. The good would then be saved and the evil damned. 'Then you'll be among the good people,' I said, encouragingly. She replied that she doubted there were any righteous people on the island.

The schoolhouse was well equipped with maps, computers, globes and books. It had five interconnecting rooms, which seemed a lot for the four pupils: Raymond, Ariel, Pania and Mason. Their ages ranged from four to fourteen. Mary and the two social workers were waiting for us. The child-sized chairs were arranged in a circle. Lady Myre took off her wellingtons and asked Raymond, aged four, if he'd like to see her toenails. He ran away and hid and had to be retrieved. Ariel, the other small boy, reprimanded me sharply when I inadvertently used the boys' toilet.

I struggled to understand the sense of Culture Day. Nola boiled up fat in a tin on a precarious burner. We were all given knives and we peeled the roots and cut them into chips.

'How do you spell manioc?' I asked, as the event was meant to be educational.

'I don't know,' Nola replied.

'Is it an indigenous plant?' I asked.

'I don't know,' she said again.

'Where does it grow?'

'Here, there and all around.'

'Can you mash it as well as make it into chips?'

'I suppose so, if you feel like it.'

Thus manioc. When the fat was hot, she put in the chips and they sizzled as chips do. Mary proposed that while they fried, we play games. The first was Throw the Ball. Whoever threw it must ask a question of the person chosen to catch it. She handed Lady Myre a pink fluffy ball. Lady Myre threw to Pania.

'What's your favourite colour?' she asked.

'Purple at the moment,' Pania replied then threw the ball to me.

'What's your earliest memory?'

'Being pushed in a pram,' I said. 'Facing the street and wondering where my mother and brothers had gone.'

I asked Nola the same question. Visiting her mother's grave

when she was three, she said, and began to cry. She restrained her tears and threw the ball to Lady Myre.

'What's your first memory?' she asked.

Lady Myre became discursive about a mouse on a mantelpiece and a nanny who sat on an open box of dates. 'Whoops,' she cried as she tired of the game and threw the ball in the air. It landed in the bubbling fat. The children perked up. The two youngest became unruly, dashed off, and were again retrieved. One of the social workers fished the ball out of the pan. It was no longer pink and fried fluff mixed with the chips.

Mary produced a sparkling wand and progressed to the Truth Game. She explained the rules. Whoever held the wand would be questioned. Their replies must be truthful, the wand would know if lies were told. I remembered a similar game one New Year's Eve with questions of a sexual sort: When did you last masturbate? Where's the strangest place you've had sex? ... I was handed the wand. A social worker, Barbara, a tall woman with hair too long for her age, had rehearsed her questions. Had I written a book called *Selkirk's Island*? ... Would I tell them about this book and show them this island on the wall map?

The intention of Culture Day was plain. I used the wand as a pointer to show the children where Juan Fernandez was on the map of the world and its position in relation to their own island. I explained how a Scottish mariner called Alexander Selkirk came to be marooned there more than two hundred years ago, after a row with the captain of his ship, how he was alone for four years before a ship of rescue came, how at first he was depressed, but then he worked to survive, how a writer called Daniel Defoe then wrote a book called *Robinson Crusoe* inspired by Selkirk's experiences...

The children were perhaps more interested in Juan Fernandez than in the bubbling chips. I put the truth wand down and asked the smallest boy, the four-year-old, what ten things he'd take with him if such a marooning happened to him. He said he'd take his toys and his teddy bear, but then he became coolly practical. He was an island boy, a survivor. He'd take a tent, a cooking pot, a sleeping bag, a knife, wire and hooks for fishing, matches, boots, a hammer, his cat called JJ to catch the rats. The other children took up the theme, the wand forgotten. Raymond said he'd take a gun, various tools for boat-building, and his guitar. Pania said she couldn't survive without her collection of rock music.

'You'd want to take a notebook wouldn't you?' Barbara said to me, 'so that you could write about your experiences and sell the serial rights for megabucks.' Was I going to write about Pitcairn? Wanda, the other social worker, asked. I said I didn't know. Maybe. But I wasn't quite sure how.

The manioc chips were drained and there was a desultory picking at them. They tasted of potato. 'I've been rumbled,' I said to Lady Myre as we walked back to Rosie's house.

She was thrilled. 'It's wonderful,' she said. 'They're bound to get us off the island now. I knew you'd be my saviour.'

Wayne was waiting. He looked official. Was I a writer? he asked.

'You could find out from the internet,' I told him. He'd

checked. I'd written about Selkirk's island and sundry women of whom he hadn't heard. 'Are you going to write about the trials?' he asked. 'Are you going to sell your story to the papers?'

I said I wasn't a journalist. I didn't know how to talk to him about chaos theory and Christian's coconut, and Rosie's blouse, and Lady Myre, and my own loss of certainties. He seemed too directional.

He told me he wanted me off the island. He feared either I or Lady Myre might get shot. He'd made further enquiries about ships. The *Buzzard Bay* would call on 30 September, bound for Panama. Two cruise ships, the *Princess* and the *Emerald*, might be persuaded to divert on their way to Easter Island.

'Hooray,' Lady Myre said, then talked of Sir Roland's connections. I said Panama wasn't convenient and that I'd rather Auckland or Tahiti.

Such suspicion made me feel guilty. It was feared I'd quiz little children and the frail elderly for revelations of a sexual sort. 'Perhaps there's room in the prison for me too,' I joked.

When he left, the atmosphere was strained. I'd been less than candid, but nothing about the place invited candour. I thought again of all the things the island didn't have: a hotel, café or bar, classes in anything useful, a cinema or theatre, and of how destructive and undermining for everyone these trials seemed to be.

We splashed to church in wellingtons with a change of shoes in bags. Rosie wore the Fenwicks blouse. She hoicked at it, wanting to make it respectable. I wore my better Rohan waistcoat and drawstring trousers. Lady Myre started out in white, with a silver sequined shawl.

The *Bounty* Bible had a notice beside it saying it must not be photographed: photos could be bought at the museum. There were a dozen varnished wooden benches, a table with a lace cloth and a vase of sparse flowers, a painting of a Pitcairn cliff face with palm trees, the pounding surf, and THE LORD IS MY ROCK AND MY SALVATION in capitals in the sky. Edward Young's great-great-great-granddaughter sat at the simplest of electric organs, there were two speakers fixed to the wall, there was a reckoner of the day's hymns: 127, 378, 130.

The congregation was small: all the visitors and six islanders. Hank began by thanking God for the day and for bringing Lady Myre and me safely to the island, then pondered the divine motive for making it impossible to unload the supplies. The prison's perimeter fence was now in Antwerp and it would cost £100,000 for a ship to bring it back to Pitcairn.

We sang the first hymn, 'Guide Me, O Thou Great Jehovah'. The first verse was delivered in near unison ordinarily enough:

> Guide me, O thou Great Jehovah,
> Pilgrim through this barren land;
> I am weak, but thou art mighty;
> Hold me with thy powerful hand.

Then came the refrain, and Lady Myre took off. The mood focused. Other thoughts were impossible. Had it been the Shaw Savill Line, neighbouring ships might have turned course in wonder:

> Bread of heaven, bread of heaven,
> Feed me till I want no more;
> Feed me till I want no more.

Suzanne couldn't match her, there weren't enough stops on her organ. Into Lady Myre's singing went the passion of her plight, and the force of her voice was extraordinary.

Hank's sermon was about the dire consequences that awaited those who disobeyed the strictures of the Sabbath. He was a handsome man with characteristic Polynesian features, though his frame was tall and slight: olive skin, dark hair and eyes, flat nose. God had punished his daughter with appendicitis after she took a Sabbath swim at St Paul's Point; his father had loaded his boat on a Saturday morning and the goat had three kids that died; his mother made a fish stew, so the well burst and they lost their water supply; Hank chopped wood and two days later his wife fell off a rock and broke her ankle; Barbara hung out her washing and Ray got a middle-ear infection. The list was long of God's retribution, of the correlating of random events, of an imaginative assumption of cause and effect. Was it, I wondered, religion, chaos theory, or just bad science without requisite tests and trials? I mused on how flexible it was, the idea of what caused what.

We moved to all six verses of 'Amazing Grace' and again Lady Myre's performance was extravagant:

> Amazing grace how sweet the sound
> That saved a wretch like me!
> I once was lost, but now am found,
> Was blind, but now I see.

She departed on an unnerving descant of her own devising,

and alarmingly stressed the words 'wretch', 'lost', and 'blind'. No creature could have been more incongruous on Pitcairn Island and I wondered at the strange accident of dispersal that had landed her there.

As we walked down the lane together Rosie commented that Lady Myre had a voice in her.

'Yes,' I said, with 'Bread of heaven' resounding in my head. I sensed Rosie was longing to get out of her blouse and into normal clothes. I wanted to tell her to use it as a shoe cloth, that it didn't matter, I'd made a mistake, not known where I was going, what to expect, or what she'd like, want or need.

She talked of the islanders' conversion to Adventism. Of the two Seventh Day Adventist evangelists in the Napa Valley, who in 1876 read of the *Bounty* story and the Pitcairners. They filled a box with religious tracts and sailed from San Francisco in a schooner called *St John*. It was the first of six crusades. All the Pitcairners converted within days. They were baptised, they repented of all sin and agreed to live by the Ten Commandments. The pigs were shoved over the cliffs: pork was forbidden, so was shellfish, alcohol, tobacco, drugs, homosexuality, bestiality, abortion and sex outside marriage. But the big thing about Adventism was the imminent Second Coming of Christ, when the righteous dead would be resurrected to meet up with the living righteous and Him. Sinners would stay dead for another thousand years. This coming was supposed to have happened in 1884, but Rosie thought it could be any day now.

She regretted that the island had no resident pastor at this difficult time and feared there might be a move against Adventism. There was talk of a Church of England pastor being sent to Pitcairn. These were uncertain times and none of them knew what the future held. But for the present it was boring when only Hank or Michael Young preached the sermon every week. Perhaps I'd like to have a go at it. Or Lady Myre.

37

I wondered if I'd turn out to be one of those strange travellers who holed up on the island from time to time and shaped its random destiny. Like John Buffett, a twenty-six-year-old shipwright from Bristol. He arrived on a whaling ship in 1823. Within eight weeks he'd married Dorothy Young and taken over as pastor in the church and sole teacher in the school.

Five years later a pseudo-aristocratic English scoundrel called George Nobbs arrived. He forced the islanders to serve him, flogged them with a cat-o'-nine-tails, made them forfeit their land if they fornicated, fathered two illegitimate children and became alcoholic on liquor from a still he devised.

Or there was Hettie André, who in 1893 sailed from the Napa Valley, set up a Seventh Day Adventist school, taught the islanders basket-weaving and wood-carving, discouraged them from dancing and made them wear long-sleeved blouses to cover up their arms.

Unsuitable people became heroes and leaders. I'd seen in the Greenwich Maritime Museum that an amnesty had been granted to John Adams in 1825 because of all he was deemed to have contributed to the Pitcairn community. I wondered about the content of my sermon. Perhaps I might talk about my mother's demise and the interruption of the linear narrative of my life with Verity. Or I might tell the congregation that they were living in the chaos of postmodernism and that the Jesus myth was obsolete. I'd advise them to leave the past behind, think of the island as a microcosm and try to create a place of fairness, a paradise of the world. Then I'd say, 'Turn to hymn number 398: "Lift up your hearts, lift up your voice".'

Lady Myre was in my bed under the net, moping. She said she was desperate to go home. It was all too much, going to church on Saturday and eating coconut pudding, which was bad for her cholesterol count, instead of lemon sorbet. She'd missed five consecutive instalments of *Sex and the City* and she wanted to sit in a restaurant and have a proper meal with waiters serving her. She said she pined for a dressed crab in Wheeler's. She wanted to hang up her clothes, soak in a bath, talk on the phone to her friends, sleep in a comfortable bed, have the papers delivered. I told her she could get *Sex and the City* on DVD, and that one of the good things about travel was that home seemed so special when, after many adventures, one at last returned there.

Barbara invited everyone on the island to a party for her seventieth birthday. She was from Florida. Six years back she'd been on a cruise that stopped at Pitcairn for two hours, and she'd spent the time talking to Charles Young. On its return from Easter Island to Auckland the ship stopped again. They talked for another two hours, he then flew to Florida, they married in the Little Church with the Big Heart and together travelled back to Pitcairn.

Between them they had seven children from previous marriages. The shack they lived in looked as if it had been trashed by an intruder determined to find a small, well-concealed piece of evidence. Neither of them seemed to mind the chaos. Barbara talked to herself in a quiet, conversational tone. Charles was distinguished by having inhaled a cockroach while snorkelling. He said it was still lodged in his lung ten years later.

The party was held in a daughter's house. All the island's women took food for it and two big tables were loaded with goat stew, chicken stew, chips, pizza, rice, pasta, salads, broccoli, mashed squash, green-banana pilhi, arrowroot pudding, pumpkin pie, jelly, cheesecake, chocolate biscuits, gluten patties and coconut-meringue pie. There was fruit juice to drink and the bare light bulbs seemed bright. No one smoked.

Lady Myre piled a plate with raspberry jelly then sprinkled the contents of her flask over it. 'Are you Randy?' she asked a large man in a T-shirt with a PITCAIRN ISLAND logo, then gave her explosive laugh. He turned away. The women stayed in one room, the men sat on the verandah and the children scuttled around.

I sat next to Steve and a man he called Sambo. They told me stories of their prowess. Steve had once caught a shark at the jetty and when he cut it open in its gut was a whole goat that must have fallen off the cliff into the sea. They boasted of catching 140 fish in an hour from a small boat, with a wire and a hook, and of goading a whale into the harbour and

jumping on its back. The island was their playground. I commended Steve on Dr Scantlebury's rescue. He shrugged. 'It's
just what we do,' he said.

I imagined the island men boasting of sexual conquest with
the same lightheartedness as they boasted of the fish they
hooked or the rats they shot. Their reference was not to the
sensibilities of other and, as they saw it, lesser creatures, it was
to the force of the sea and the thrill of conquest. They looked
like mutineers, like pirates. They didn't go to church or consider Judgement Day. Their strength worked the long boats,
felled trees, built houses and the prison and rescued a drowning man in a storm. They resented intruders who assumed
moral superiority and told them how they should behave.

I asked Steve about shipping and he laughed. Eight months
was the longest without a ship coming by, he told me. It had
never been worse than now.

Often I trudged the island: to Garnet's Ridge, Ginger Valley,
Flat Land, Up the Beans and Down Rope, and always with a
sense of being watched. There were few creatures to observe –
only cats, rats, geckos, chickens and seabirds. On a day when
the sun shone I searched for the giant tortoise, Mrs T, but
didn't find her. I walked to my favourite place at St Paul's Point
where the waves pounded more fiercely and with brighter
spray than ever I'd seen. Faint spray fluttered over me and I
wrote in my notebook of island things: how a shark washed up
on the rocks was thought to be dead until it bit off someone's
hand, how Pawl, the biggest, fiercest-looking man on Pitcairn,
was one of the few untainted by sexual wrongdoing. He'd

shaved his head and was covered in tattoos. Around his neck he wore pendants of a shark's tooth, a black pearl, a shell, a piece of horn. He'd pierced his ears with many holes by jabbing them against a spike, and he'd made the rings he threaded through.

I looked up to see Bea and two men observing me. They hesitated, but kept to their plan and clambered with barefoot ease to the lower rocks to fish. They stood in the spume of the waves, cracked fish dead and threw them into a basket. I called to ask what they'd caught. Bea held up a brightly coloured fish. There was nanwee, grouper, parrot, wrasse, but the friendliness was formal. I was an intruder.

I walked on. Much of the land was eroded. Where once there'd been pineapple plots and banana trees, now there were stretches of empty red soil, or rose apple bushes fit only for firewood. I passed Nola's house. She was baking bread on wood embers in a stone oven. I sensed her reserve and left. At the prison, Hank was spreading the gravel path and Pania was filling nail holes round the trim of the doors. I admired the tongue-and-groove of the walls, the light fittings, the shower rooms. I wondered if the potential prisoners building their own cells had devised some way of ensuring escape. Foolishly I asked this and again met with discouraging politeness.

In the museum were motley relics displayed in rickety glass cases: bits of broken wood and ballast, a cannonball and rock-encrusted rope, all apparently from the *Bounty*; copies of all postage stamps printed for the island; a set of Victorian scales for weighing letters; an old mould for making a hat; photos of Graham Wragg counting bird bones; photos of tourists arriving at the other islands in the Pitcairn group, Henderson, Ducie and Oeno; photos of girls in the Adventist school, covered neck to ankle in white muslin uniforms.

On the board by the courtroom was an edict that all firearms must be handed in by 7 September. Failure to comply would result in 'the enactment of an ordinance to enforce their surrender'. A letter of response from the islanders said they needed their guns to shoot down breadfruit and coconuts from the trees and that this was one more act of interference.

At her house Rosie was talking to Lady Myre about living in a state of fallen grace and how Lucifer was once an angel. The policemen sat at the table eating eggs, chips and chocolate pudding. I checked my email. Nothing from Verity. Mother had told the staff at Sunset View that her children had conspired to have her imprisoned there.

Rosie assigned the Saturday sermon to Lady Myre. She'd failed to interest her in banana-drying, or anything much, and seemed to feel her discontent as a reflection on herself as host.

Lady Myre took to the idea but wanted an audience. On the Shaw Savill Line she'd played to a packed theatre every night, she said. And in *No Sex, Please, We're British* the queue for returns in Huddersfield had stretched halfway down Queen's Street. 'Bums on seats,' she said, 'that's what's needed.' There was a reason why the theatres were full and the churches empty: people were having a better time at the theatre. As for the Bible, she'd been incarcerated by herself in enough hotel rooms with iffy TVs to know it wasn't an easy read. How could you get excited about a book called Leviticus? All that wrath of God and plagues.

She called her sermon 'The Second Coming'. I asked if that was a good idea in the light of the current sex charges. She said I was a naughty mousey. She printed out a flyer and we delivered it to all the houses:

THE SECOND COMING
11 a.m.
Come to Church this Saturday and hear Lady Myre's
Views on this Perennial Problem.
Lady Myre is not Representative of Any Known Religion.
Free Gifts, Singing, Dancing.

None of the defendants showed up. I wondered if they feared a stitch-up. The policemen sat in the back row and looked more formal than usual. Wayne was there and his wife. Hank began with church business: the times of forthcoming Bible studies, the rota for polishing the pews. Lady Myre was late and the pre-school-age children restive. Her entrance was calculated. She wore a sort of *tunica alba* and a headpiece that seemed like a cross between a mitre and a bicycle helmet. She looked like Edna Everidge impersonating a bishop. She distributed tambourines and maracas and offered what she called 'a warm warm welcome', then took off with the song 'Lord, I'm Coming Home':

> Coming home, coming home, never more to roam;
> Open wide thine arms of love, Lord, I'm coming home.

As ever, she brought more than herself to the situation. The mood grew lively, though uncontrolled, and Damian who was three, became overzealous with his tambourine. He couldn't be dissuaded from banging and rattling it inappropriately, then cried at an effort to take it from him.

Her sermon was disappointing: anecdotal and discursive. She went on about meeting Sir Roland on Riis Beach. I noted that the story changed with retelling and the frenzied Pekinese stealing the bathing hat had become a Yorkshire terrier. 'I believe in destiny,' Lady Myre said. '*Che sera sera*, whatever will be will be.' She started singing again in her operatic soprano. The bewildered congregation joined in, 'The future's not ours to see. Che sera sera.'

I pondered the confusion of opposed ideas: God, or no God, chance or predetermination, chaos or linear narrative. Not for the first time I felt relief at the one certainty of death. Lady Myre talked of her search for her half-brother. Once again I doubted the existence of a Garth or a Sir Roland. She said perhaps she was a second coming. Why else would she have holed up in such a peculiar place? She always travelled with Explore where everything was done for one. All she'd ever wanted was to spread a little happiness. She jiggled from side to side with the palms of her hands facing us:

> Even when the darkest clouds are in the sky
> You mustn't sigh and you mustn't cry,
> Spread a little happiness as you go by.

There were guffaws from the congregation, murmurs and shuffling. Lady Myre was undeterred. There'd been, she said, in her country England a very wonderful lady prime minister, the first ever, who was inspired by Saint Francis of Assisi:

> Where there is hatred let me sow love,

179

Where there is darkness, light,
Where there is sadness, joy.

That, Lady Myre said, was how she felt too. Then she led the singing for another of her gospel songs, if that's what they were:

We're little black sheep who've gone astray,
    Baa-aa-aa!
Gentlemen wankers out on the spree,
Damned from here to Eternity.
God ha' mercy on such as we,
    Bah! Yah! Bah!

Then it got out of hand. There was worse than murmuring from the visitors, and Damian couldn't be constrained on his pew. He marched up and down, banged and rattled his tambourine and shouted 'Baa! Yah! Bah!' I heard the word 'Blasphemy'. The two policemen moved to help Lady Myre from the platform. Did we know, she shouted, that those lines were composed by the famous English poet Rudyard Kipling? 'That's enough,' Ed the Scottish policeman said and took her arm.

'Wait,' she said. She scooped a handful of beads from a white bag and threw them into the congregation, such as it was. There was a shriek from one of the social workers, who thought they were a sort of explosive. The beads rolled down the aisle and along the pews. Nola and the children scrambled for them. Lady Myre was hurried from the church. 'Hands off, young man,' she said. 'I'm Lady Myre.'

The islanders went home. I congratulated her on a spirited performance.

'Was I moving?' she asked.

'Intriguing,' I said. 'But it's gentlemen *rankers*, not wankers.'

She looked nonplussed and said she knew a fair number of wankers but what were the others? I told her I believed they were officers who'd been promoted from the ordinary ranks of foot soldiers. She said Roley's friend Sir Anthony Polworth had taught her the words and he had a soft 'r'.

Over lunch of pickfish and sweet potatoes Rosie's good cheer seemed forced. Hank ate in silence. I feared they were offended. I talked of general things: ham radio links, the dried-banana business, but they remained wary and reserved, as if any exchange of niceties might be a trap.

And then it happened. Early one September morning after a night of bugs, the usual ghostly visiting from Lady M. and concern over when a ship might call, over the intercom came a man's voice with a German accent. 'My name is Kurt. I am a lone yachtsman. I am from Switzerland. I need to land. I need water and to purchase supplies.' He'd anchored, and he gave his bearings and asked if a boat would come out to pick him up.

I knocked on Rosie and Hank's bedroom door. They'd heard the news on the speaker beside their bed. 'Steve will deal with it,' Rosie said. Both seemed uninterested in yet another tourist floating past on a casual journey, wanting something.

I climbed to Garnet's Ridge and across the bay saw the yacht, a small, bright white speck, bobbing with the tide. It looked more like drifting polystyrene than a ship of rescue. Hours later I found Kurt by the Breadfruit Fence. He was tall and strong-looking, wore glasses and was deeply tanned by the wind, sea and sun. No one had gone out to his boat to fetch him. He'd waited until light then taken his dinghy to the jetty. He'd sailed from Antwerp, hadn't spoken for forty-nine days, and he wanted a beer and a cigarette.

I explained why Pitcairn was a dry island, the conversion to Seventh Day Adventism, how cigarettes weren't sold, there was no café, and liquor couldn't be drunk without a licence. I said I knew of an islander who might help him out.

Lady Myre scuttled up, breathless with anticipation. She hugged Kurt extravagantly and called him her saviour, her vision of wonder. He looked perplexed, having been alone for all those days. 'Where are you *going*?' she asked. Mangareva, he said. To meet with his friend Wilhelm. And then to American Samoa. 'Take me,' she said. 'You must get me off.' She told him how nightly she was bitten by bugs, of her fear of going to the bathroom because of spiders as big as her hands and the sound of scuttling mice, of land crabs that crunched cockroaches, of being stung on the bottom by nesting wasps, how the men on the island were sex offenders who peered through her window hoping to molest her, how her husband Sir Roland Myre had run the Admiralty, how she'd never wanted to go to Pitcairn at all but had been grotesquely deceived by a shipping agent.

It all poured out in a torrent. Some of it was not as I'd remembered, but her desperation was real. Pitcairn was not to her liking. It occurred to me it must be strange for this man who'd been so long alone to have silence broken by this tirade. He asked if I had similar problems. I said, 'Not quite,' but that I too would like to travel with him, if he'd agree, because I didn't know how else I'd ever get off the island. I explained about the *Braveheart*, plying to and from Mangareva bringing judges and lawyers and policemen to Pitcairn, and how it was chartered by special licence to the British government and couldn't take tourists. Kurt said he'd consider the legal and insurance implications and let us know the following day. I took him to Pawl's house and procured eight cigarettes and two cans of lager. He was startled by Pawl's multiple ear-piercings, extravagant tattoos and shaven head, and I wanted to tell him that here was a kind and gentle man, with a talent for making jewellery and an enthusiasm for books.

Ed the policeman came in, though it was still only about nine in the morning. Word had got round that the two Englishwomen and the lone yachtsman were together. He needed to check it all out. He took Kurt away on his quad bike. Lady Myre said she was going to her room to light a candlenut and say a novena to Erasmus, the patron saint of boatmen.

Next morning Kurt called to say he was sorry but he couldn't risk it. Wayne wanted me and Lady Myre off the island but had warned him if he took tourists he might have his boat impounded by the French customs at Mangareva and be fined twenty thousand dollars. He needed to get to Samoa and then to Australia to meet up with his sister.

Lady Myre's eyes rolled. She rocked and keened and said she'd die on Pitcairn and that God was punishing her. Her clothes were covered in red mud, the lights went off at ten at night, there were no shops, no television, no newspapers, no servants. She was dying for a cup of real coffee. Sex offenders peered at her through lit windows, her husband was in the Admiralty...

So Kurt agreed to take us. I had to admire (and not for the first or last time) how adept she was at having her way. He coached us to say to the Mangarevan authorities that we were friends of his from Basle, we'd arranged to meet him at Pitcairn, we weren't paying passengers.

His boat, called *Luceann* after his children Ludovic, Cedric and Annette, was, he said, the Mercedes Benz of yachts – none better, built in Perpignan to a very high specification and with great attention to detail. Though Lady Myre and I must share a cabin, we'd have all comforts: reading lamps, a hot shower, a flush toilet... He'd checked the weather forecast with Hank. We must be down at the jetty by ten the following morning.

It was a day of packing and hasty goodbyes. I tried not to communicate the excitement I felt, not to inspire dissatisfaction in those compelled to stay. I couldn't believe those mutineers and deceived Polynesians – young, strong and at home on the sea – would have stayed in this cut-off place. If they'd had the chance to leave on a small boat on an uncertain journey to an unknown destination, they'd have taken it. And it seemed understandable that the women, after the men had gone, would tear down a house to build a boat to follow in their wake.

That last night, long past the time when the generator was switched off, Rosie, Hank, Michael Young and I talked by candlelight. They all lived by their Adventist beliefs. I thought how brazen evangelical religion was – how it imposed certainties and took away customs and doubts. It seemed strange to expect retribution for baking a cake on a certain day.

They talked of their fears for the future if the jetty wasn't built and shipping improved. The island was being turned into a prison. They felt they missed out on the benefits of British citizenship but were penalised by the disadvantages, and they wondered what other charges might be levelled against them. They'd no knowledge of the intricacies of British law. Only in 1970 had they been given British passports and citizenship. Before that their passports, issued in Fiji, stipulated their right to reside on Pitcairn.

They were worried by a piecemeal approach to the island, with no rounded vision for reform. All the problems intertwined: erosion, a non-existent infrastructure, a small, ageing population, lack of money. A government official had been sent to eradicate the rose apple that choked indigenous plants. When it was ripped out there was further erosion of the soil. The tradition of barter had worked in the past but now there were too few islanders, and resources were depleted. Money couldn't be made out of selling honey, dried bananas and curios if no ships called. Nor could they compete on prices. The cost of drying bananas was high. The generator was driven by diesel transported at prohibitive cost. It would be cheaper to give them money and save the electricity.

Hank said, like Rosie, that he'd missed out on his daughters' childhood. After they'd gone away to school in New Zealand they'd never really come home to Pitcairn in spirit. And Rosie now missed out on her role as a grandmother. But over and above everything was the trouble of these trials. The cost was so high. And what would it buy them but grief?

IV

LEAVING PITCAIRN

Chaos imposes limitation upon our ability to forecast

38

We grouped by the jetty. The wind was a light west-north-westerly. 'Perfect,' Kurt said. 'We'll be in Mangareva in thirty-six hours. Two hundred and sixty nautical miles. Seven knots an hour.' To me the sea looked wintry and rough. 'The sea's sweet,' Hank said. 'The wind will catch your sails.'

Rosie'd taken me to the shore on her quad bike and I was spattered with mud. A clutch of Pitcairners was there to say goodbye: all four of the island's schoolchildren, Nola with a bag of pineapple buns, Hank with a crate of cabbages, bananas, grapefruit, clementines, pawpaws, yams and passion fruit – 'for the journey,' he said and would take no money. Bea rested a spear with a crab wriggling on its spike against the jetty wall and stamped my passport. 'Welcome to the Pitcairn Islands, Police and Immigration'. It seemed a contrary stamp, as I was leaving, but everything Pitcairn seemed contrary. 'B. Christian Police Officer,' she wrote beneath it in curly writing.

Lady Myre had been there since dawn. She was dressed for the sea, the logo FIRST MATE on her T-shirt, her visor white, her mascara blue, her shorts patterned with anchors. Her elegant legs were peppered with bug bites and mud. Round her neck were a spyglass and compass, clipped to her belt was her flask of rum and pawpaw juice. Her fourteen pieces of luggage stacked by the jetty all bore what I supposed was the Myre crest – a dragon at odds with a pitchfork. 'My man,' she called to Kurt. He gave an embarrassed smirk. 'Ship ahoy,' she called, and waved at the catamaran as it bounced on the waves in Bounty Bay.

Kurt took her luggage and my small rucksack ahead in the dinghy. I hovered, waiting for his return, anticipating separation from the islanders. The visiting officials were arrayed, pleased I was leaving with my views unpenned. Mary, orchestrator of the Truth Game, gave me a triumphant peck. 'Back to Hampstead, eh?' She looked, as ever, pleased with what she said. Les, the locum, talked of seasickness remedies, his nice wife smiled. The social workers stood about looking like social workers, the two policemen looked bored.

I hugged Rosie and told her I'd miss her. 'How well we hit it off,' I said, 'two women from such different backgrounds.' She said she'd miss me too. I thanked her for all her many kindnesses. She thanked me for the blouse and gave me a letter she'd written to her Chinese friend Charles Mo in Mangareva. Perhaps he'd help me find accommodation there, she said.

Lady Myre tripped from the jetty to the dinghy and Kurt's arms with a whoop and an ooh-la-la. I stepped down decorously with merely a steadying hand. We sped out to sea and I waved: at the small group on the jetty, at the Hill of Difficulty and Bang Iron Valley, at this isolated, troubled island to which I'd never return, at some inner melancholy, at a half-imagined image of that bedraggled group of fugitives who'd arrived there in January 1790, desperate for fresh water and the peaceful cover of trees. Most of all I waved at Rosie, though I soon could not see her wide, smiling face. Those abducted Polynesian women, Mauatua, Faahotu, Mareva, Teatuahitea, were with her, in her work, in her cooking, in her dark skin and hair, in her knowledge of the island and the Pitcairn dialect. I hadn't intended to leave when I did, or in this hurried way, I regretted I'd not been to Henderson Island or seen the flight-less rail, but it had seemed serendipitous when I heard Kurt's voice on the intercom and saw his yacht on the ocean.

'Bye-bye, Bounty Bay,' Lady Myre called. She flicked extravagant kisses from her fingertips then turned to the virgin territory of Kurt, her ascent from the dinghy to his boat, and her journey into the blue.

There were three cabins. Kurt had the largest with a control panel by his bed. The second was taken up with yellow oil-skins and all Lady Myre's luggage. The bed to which she and I were consigned took up most of the third. 'Queen size,' said Kurt. There were two windows close to the sea, which could be opened if it was calm.

'Mmm,' said Lady Myre. 'What fun. Are you for aft or star-board?' She wheeled in a case the size of a cupboard. 'I don't want much for the voyage,' she said, then whispered, 'So we're bed-mates after all.'

Kurt pulled the anchor, hoisted sails and talked about main-sails and roller reefing and the wind abaft the beam. He showed us how to switch on the engine, pump the toilet, boil the kettle and blow our whistles when we fell into the sea. He explained how, if the boat flipped over in a storm, though it couldn't be righted, it was possible to survive for two weeks in a watertight cell in the cabin.

He fired the engine. Pitcairn receded to a grey strip on the horizon. Within a month it would break into the world's news, an isolated rock defined by its desperate past and the vast

Pacific Ocean, its menfolk shamed, its people uncertain what citizenship they held or from where help might come. Kurt bounded the deck. I sat at the ship's wheel and he switched from autopilot to manual and told me to watch the dials and keep the course on twenty-nine. It was as near as I would ever come to navigation. I felt exhilarated as I steered the waves, at one with the sea, the wind and the sky. I was an eighteenth-century mariner on the wide southern sea, there was nothing in view but the circle of the world, a frigate bird, a tern, a distant wave's crest that might be mistaken for a ship.

Lady Myre swayed on to the deck holding a carrier bag. She was the colour of Kermit and her mouth was fixed in a rictus. 'Sick,' she said, then lay on the floor. Both she and I were wearing transdermal patches of Scopoderm behind our ears, and acupressure wristbands, and had swallowed quantities of Stugeron. I felt scornful of her for not being more of a sailor, for not being able to transcend such visceral things. I felt an intense sense of freedom on this small boat and on such a journey of chance. Close to the sea and the wind and sails, I imagined the *Bounty* cutting its lonely course, with the mutineers searching for the uncharted island of Pitcairn. I imagined Captain Bligh and the other eighteen men plying the ocean in that launch half the size of this boat, living on an ounce of bread and a quarter of a pint of water a day. Kurt cut out the engine and the wind caught the sails. This, I felt, was the true experience of the sea.

But suddenly, too, my body felt cold and a wave of nausea made me groan. 'Keep busy,' Kurt said. 'Don't give in to it. It's

all in the mind. Keep your eyes on the ocean.' He said he was
starving and asked me if I'd like fried eggs and sausages. I
made it to the toilet but couldn't recall what to do with the
levers. Kurt ignored me. I returned to the deck and lay beside
Lady Myre. Her eyes didn't register. My teeth juddered. I
didn't mind if I were to die. She held my hand. 'What an adventure,' she whispered with a slur. 'Isn't it corking?' A smell
of fatty sausage wafted by. 'Aren't we lucky ones?' she said, 'I
wouldn't miss this for worlds.' Then she threw up again.

Time seemed to stop. I was aware of Kurt moving the sails, of
the sky darkening as the world turned. At some point he suggested we'd be more comfortable in the cabin, but neither of
us moved. At night he covered us with blankets and oilskins.
I dozed and woke and saw wave after wave furled with white.
I saw the moon emerge from clouds. Beyond the awfulness of
it all I felt glad to be on this small craft. I heard the music of
the ocean in a timeless night and felt the thread between then
and now. I thought of Bligh and his crew and how the sea had
washed over them and they'd bailed all through their dark
nights. I imagined them throwing valued stores overboard so
they could bail better and to lighten the boat: clothes, rope,
spare sails... I thought of the lies told to Titahiti, Manarii,
Oheu and the other Polynesian men trapped on the *Bounty* in
a chaotic venture they couldn't control. And the animals – the
pigs, goats and hens – and their bewildered suffering on a
journey to hell.

So Lady Myre and I spent our night together, prone on deck.
Even in the dark she looked weird, her nose very small, her

mouth very wide. She'd wrapped a jersey round her face to protect her ears from the wind. At one point she sang in her clear soprano, 'Oh Mr Porter, what shall I do? / I wanted to go to Birmingham and you've taken me on to Crewe,' and then convulsed with laughter, which made her head hurt and her stomach retch. I said I thought she'd wanted to go to Picton. 'Yes,' she said, 'that's what happens, you start out intending one thing and you end up with another.' I hadn't the energy to remind her of my interest in chaos theory, and how small initial differences amplify until they are no longer small, and of the order that lies behind chaos but is not providential.

The following afternoon, feeling better, we sat with Kurt in the cockpit lounge and sipped peppermint tea. But the weather had gone haywire, I suppose because of unknown variables. The predicted wind direction was spectacularly wrong and we were being blown due north by force seven winds at thirty knots an hour, with gusts of fifty knots and waves forty feet high. Kurt said it didn't matter because there was no land to crash into before Alaska. He didn't want to pitch into the wind or use his limited fuel, so he hove to, reefed the sails, pulled up the dagger boards, turned off the autopilot and said we'd go where we would and wait for the weather to change.

There were terrible cracks and bangs as the sea pounded the boat. Lady Myre said she wanted something stronger than tea. She'd finished her rum, so I got my flask of Glenfiddich from my bag. She added cranberry juice to hers to hide the taste, though I told her I doubted this was a good idea. Our glasses swooped across the table.

'Let's talk about sexual organs,' Kurt said. I said I'd rather not. 'He's a dry stick,' Lady Myre whispered. 'The slightest spark will ignite him. Cross your legs and hunch your shoulders.'

Kurt then went to the cockpit door and yelled, 'You bloody bitch.' I feared I was very much at sea with two extremely strange people. 'Bloody fucking Pacific,' he said. 'If I'd've known it would be like this, I'd never have come here.' Then he sat and delivered a monologue, for he hadn't spoken for all those days. He said he'd lived on this boat for four years, had given up a lucrative veterinary practice in Basle and never again wanted a house. He'd left his wife because he was in love with his receptionist. For a year they hadn't touched, but the atmosphere between them as they tended the Chihuahuas and wolfhounds had been electric, all day, and day after day.

'Dear oh dear,' said Lady Myre. A huge wave broke over the deck. Her open case slid across the cabin floor.

He realised he'd never loved his wife but he needed a woman and didn't want to sail alone. He was now forty-nine and his moods veered from depression to elation. When young he'd read Nietzsche and thought of suicide. His father's tyrannical moods had ruled the house and his mother was subservient to him – he'd died twenty-six years ago of prostate cancer. She was now eighty, Valium-addicted and with her memory shot to pieces. She didn't know Kurt was alone on the ocean, she thought he was with his last girlfriend Leila, who was Brazilian and black and had no money and was so beautiful she was stared at in all the ports. She had three children, all with different fathers, and had deceived Kurt into thinking they were her brother's children. She used to leave her knickers on the windlass and the rigging.

'Dear oh dear,' said Lady Myre once more. The sky was black with rain, and lightning forked the ocean. Kurt went outside and again shouted, 'You fucking bitch.' I was afraid he'd be washed overboard, leaving Lady Myre and me alone to manage the boat.

The wind, now gale force nine, moaned, and blue-black waves, fringed with white and high like mountains, cracked against the boat. Lady Myre lurched to the cabin, I supposed to be sick again. I refrained from mentioning the cranberry juice. Kurt said sailing was a metaphor for freedom, and the ocean helped him formulate his thoughts and to find himself. I thought of the *Bounty* and of being cooped up. I felt I had a better understanding of why they might have massacred each other when the opportunity came. Once again Kurt asked me if I'd like a sausage. He got out a packet of bright-red things acquired from the Pitcairn shop. I wondered why he resisted Hank's fresh fruit and vegetables. I thought of the hunger of the ocean's sharks and of how long it might take to die of hypothermia. I had a headache and felt very strange.

'You look like an ostrich,' Kurt told me. 'You watch every wave. You go to the worst-case scenario. I am anxious, but you make me more anxious.'

Lady Myre returned, dressed as a pirate, in knee-length breeches and cummerbund, with a red-spotted kerchief round her head. She'd applied bright-red lipstick, green eyeshadow and a sickly perfume – Joy, perhaps, by Jean Patou. She lurched with the yacht, whooped and slid to a seat. 'You're very good-looking,' she said to Kurt. I said I must lie down. I felt sure they'd manage without me.

I lay on the cabin bed and watched the waves pound against the window glass. I didn't see how such a small boat could survive this pounding much longer. I hoped for a quick demise. The thought of first being cocooned with these two for a fortnight, upside down in the watertight hull of the cabin, seemed an unwelcome option. I imagined the *Pandora* as it wrecked on the barrier reef, the wailing of the wind in the rigging, the cries for help, which did not come, of the drowning men, some still in shackles.

I closed my eyes and again tried to remember the names of the mutineers with Fletcher Christian on the *Bounty* as he searched for Pitcairn: Alexander Smith, Edward Young, Matthew Quintal, William Brown. It occurred to me that I never used Lady Myre's first name and that I didn't know her unmarried name, and how bleached of meaning names become, and how hard they are to remember if they are unfamiliar sounds.

I thought of David Nelson the botanist, in that open boat with Bligh, racked by fever and gut pain and without even the comfort of a soft bed and a warm blanket, as I had now. Bligh named Nelson Hill in Tasmania after him when he stopped there in February 1792 in the *Providence* on his second breadfruit journey to Tahiti.

I tried to recite the inventory of what they had with them in the open boat: twine, sails, some bread, pieces of pork, six quarts of rum, six bottles of wine, a quadrant and compass, four cutlasses, no maps... I wondered why Christian allowed them anything. He knew what a resourceful navigator Bligh was, how fired he'd be by the challenge to survive with scant resources. Why hadn't he tipped him empty-handed into the boat to a certain death, the way people now abandon dogs on the motorways? I puzzled again about the true relationship between Christian and Bligh. Bligh had said Christian was the 'object of his particular regard and attention'. What had that meant beyond dining with him nightly and tutoring him in the ways of the sea? And what was behind that plea of Christian's: 'That Captain Bligh, that is the thing. I am in hell. I am in hell.' Bligh was quick to say the mutiny was 'not to be wondered at' because of the lure of the Tahitian women. But Christian didn't seem that enamoured of women, whatever the fiction told by Clark Gable, Marlon Brando or Mel Gibson.

My reveries soothed me, so that although I didn't forget I was being buffeted towards Alaska in dangerous seas, or how uncontrolled the situation was – that I was quite beyond reach of rescue and that no one who cared for me knew where I was – I found I could listen in a disinterested way to the thwacking of the waves. I thought of the real meaning of metaphors of the ocean – all at sea, washed up, adrift, going under – and although I felt detached from hope or prayer and had no sense of fate, as I lay still my mind calmed into the acceptance world of luck and grief and the split-second recognition of chance.

Lady Myre crept into the cabin at some indeterminate hour, shed her clothes, put on men's pyjamas – Sir Roland's perhaps – and crawled in beside me. She snuggled far too close.

She smelled of peppermint and whisky and her perfume and of the sea somehow and the outdoors. 'I know you're not asleep,' she whispered. 'Who *could* be in all this?' A mighty wave – was it the tenth? I wondered – cracked against the boat. I said nothing. I felt I was the eye of the storm inside and outside the catamaran.

'You know I'm incredibly attracted to you,' Lady Myre said. I refused to be unnerved even in this noisy dark and with the chaotic motion of the sea. With every rise of the boat to the wave's peak an eerie light strobe-lit her face. Yesterday she'd been green, tonight she was silvery white. She'd wound some sort of wires or pipe cleaners into her hair – I wasn't going to enquire why. 'Please put your hand in my jim-jams and make me come,' Lady Myre said. I lay very still and kept very quiet the way one does in the vicinity of a roused creature of an unfamiliar species whose intentions are unclear. 'Please,' she said.

In my career as a lesbian I've had a great many lovers, many of them exciting, all of them unsuitable, but I've always retained a sense of in some way choosing my destiny for the night. This night it seemed was to be an exception. I wondered if danger had made her sexual. I've heard sex is never more intense than when bomber planes fly overhead. I suggested Kurt was more up for it than I and clearly found her attractive. I said I wouldn't at all mind or feel left out if she went to him and they shared a cabin.

'You little fool,' she said. 'It's you I want. I'm more attracted to you than to anyone for years.'

I made the drear excuse of the headache, for I didn't want to offend or be unkind. In fact my headache, curiously, had disappeared and the huge capricious ocean no longer seemed my main concern, though it continued to buffet this bauble of a boat towards the most northern shore. 'Perhaps we should just lie quietly together,' I said, 'a shelter from the storm.' She made an exasperated noise but then became quiet and put her arms lightly around me. I didn't want to encourage her or be misconstrued, but out of a sort of gratitude I gently nuzzled my face against her neck.

Thus we arranged ourselves, rather as on the previous night. I was aware of the silkiness of her skin and of her thoughtful stillness. I tried not to think about the oddness of her manner, the smallness of her nose, the wideness of her mouth, her alarming changes in skin colour and the way she made me think of Hans Holbein's *Dance of Death*. In this violent night she was my consolation. Or at least she was there, unlike anyone else. The mighty ocean lifted us high then dropped us down. We had no choice but to assent to its ferocious rhythm, its repetition. Its waves pushed us hard against each other. I lay in the slight arms of this strangest of strangers and sort of had sex with the sea.

'This too will pass,' I said.

'I hope it never does,' she replied.

At some point in that timeless night I struggled to the toilet: to be sick, of course, and to have a pee. I staggered and clung to a protruding sink or jamb. There was water swilling over the floor, and the cockpit door was open. I tried to look outside for Kurt but there was just the maniacal sea. I was soaked with spray when Lady Myre hauled me back into the bunk and I told her of my fears.

'I hope he's gone,' she said. 'Then it will be just you and me and the cruel sea.'

I supposed I was afraid, but I had been more afraid, when young, of rejection, abandonment and the indifference of those whom I would have liked to love me. I did not doubt the sea's indifference on this wild night, though it seemed like involvement of the deepest sort.

I thought that perhaps, when morning came, the storm might give way to a rueful sunrise and calmer seas and the chance again to find our course, but the thwacking of the waves went on. I didn't know if Lady Myre was awake or asleep. She lay silent and still, as if *in extremis* she'd at last found calm. In the first grey light of dawn I remembered it was my birthday. I decided I wouldn't tell my companions, for it seemed irrelevant. I thought of the ordinary contentment of the previous year: Verity bringing me a cup of tea in bed, her gift of an electronic organiser, her card with a photo of migrating swallows, our supper at a fish restaurant in Borough Market. It all seemed safe and out of reach and long ago.

The storm did not abate. At dawn Kurt came to our cabin door. 'I have a very severe announcement,' he said. 'And I don't want *you*' – he jerked the word and jabbed a finger at me – 'to make things worse than they are.' He said the rudder was jammed. The force of the waves had slammed against it so he couldn't now steer, and the boat was beyond control. The only way to free it was for him to dive beneath the hull, which was impossible in these seas with waves converged in force ten winds. A wave would crack his head and kill him, and anyway he might need a jack and a wrench, which he didn't have. The wind had apparently again changed and we were now back where we'd been twelve hours previously. He said we'd have to drift until the sea was calm enough for him to dive, which might be for two weeks, and that though now we were again heading towards Pitcairn, the wind was so capricious, the sea so turbulent, all might change again and again.

I remembered Bligh's notes about how, in the open boat, when they'd got through the Great Barrier Reef and were pulling the boat ashore on a tiny uninhabited island, a gudgeon had broken from the rudder. That had been in May 1789. He wrote that, had it happened at sea, it 'would probably have been the cause of our perishing as the management of the boat could not have been so nicely preserved as these very heavy seas required'. I'd looked up 'gudgeon' in the dictionary. It was the metal socket in which the pintle of a rudder turns. I'd looked up 'pintle'. It was a pin or bolt. I supposed that the same thing had gone wrong now, but in very heavy seas.

I thought of Randy Christian and Dr Scantlebury in a small boat near the Pitcairn coast, of a wave snapping the boat like a twig, and of him dragging Scantlebury with his head bleeding into the dark cave he knew about, and of how these sorts of things were always happening to someone somewhere.

Kurt railed about the seaworthiness of his catamaran – how the mast had broken in the Mediterranean, so helicopters had to guide him in to St Tropez, and things weren't yet sorted on that because the insurers said it was his fault, but that this was worse. These were the worst seas he'd ever seen – worse than when he'd rounded the Horn. These winds were at fifty knots. They were force ten to eleven on the Beaufort scale and the swell of the waves took them forty feet high. He asked me what I'd done on Pitcairn to make the seas so violent.

I got five milligrams of Valium from my sponge bag. Kurt said the wind was again building up. I didn't see how it could build up more. I noticed he moved round the boat with his legs apart the way drunks do when trying to keep their balance. Lady Myre started to sing 'A Life on the Ocean Wave' and kept saying, 'Where *are* my chocolate brazils?' She seemed to have even more teeth and an ever wider smile. She wanted us all to play a board game. She'd found one called Dingo and another called Murder on the Orient Express. She dropped both boxes and counters scattered everywhere.

Between me and Kurt was an atmosphere of accusation. He blamed me for exacerbating things. I asked him to use his satellite phone to inform someone of our whereabouts. I said I thought it would be a consolation if someone knew where we were, and they might think of a way to help us. What 'someone' did I suggest? he asked with scorn – his sister in Frankfurt, perhaps. I volunteered the cellphone numbers of Graham Wragg on the *Bounty Bay*, and Nigel Jolly on the *Braveheart*, both of whose boats plied these seas. Or the Pitcairn Administration Office in Auckland, or a shipping agent there, or a journalist in Tauranga.

'Do you really think', Kurt asked me, 'that a small boat would divert to help us in these seas, or that anyone would send out a ship or a plane to rescue us? Do you know where we are? We're in the middle of the Pacific Ocean. Do you know the size of the Pacific Ocean?'

I very easily feel guilty, but I couldn't see how it was my fault that any of this had happened. But he went to his cabin and I heard him speaking to what must have been the Pitcairn Office in Auckland. He gave our latitude and longitude and explained our plight. He said we were 22° 51 mins south in latitude and 132° 06 mins west in longitude. He said it wasn't a Mayday – he didn't think we were in immediate danger – but we had no manoeuvrability and if the storm changed direction and we were carried at this speed towards Pitcairn's rocky coast, we'd be in real trouble. Then he went outside and I saw him sort of swinging from the rigging, and again I hoped he wouldn't be washed overboard, though he seemed a rather redundant captain as things were.

Lady Myre decided to scramble eggs, but the pan and everything else flew across the galley. She asked me if I believed in God, and I said I didn't. It seemed she'd taken little notice of all I'd told her about chaos and random but significant interactions. She said she believed in everything: God, Buddhism, Horoscopy, Love, and that belief seemed better than scepticism, because she'd rather say yes to life than no. And she gave me her terrible smile.

We ate pineapple buns and cornflakes and tried to stop the powdered-milk mix slopping out of our bowls. Kurt asked about the sex crimes on Pitcairn and, because we seemed again to be heading in that direction, I tried to voice my views about the island and citizenship and the current trials and to what law of what land or conscience a man was answerable when it came to the rape of a girl.

Lady Myre said she thought mandatory castration was the only thing to stop rapists re-offending. She said she doubted there was such a thing as good sex on Pitcairn and, as far as she was concerned, good sex was defined by the intensity of her orgasm. 'If on the Richter scale', she said, 'it's of magnitude nine, and ricochets through me, whoosh whoosh whoosh whoosh, then I call that good sex whatever the technique.' She'd found her chocolate brazils and was sharing them with Kurt. She was wearing an emerald-green visor and matching shorts and a purple T-shirt with the slogan DIESEL printed across it. With a wink she told me these were the colours of women's emancipation.

Kurt wanted to pursue this line of conversation but I did not. I told him how the estimated cost of the Pitcairn trials was more than five million pounds but very little money was spent on this remote island's infrastructure. How they depended on rain for the water supply and hadn't a proper jetty or café or mainland phone. How they were all related to each other and that with few visitors they were suspicious of the outside world and how these troubles divided families and humiliated them all.

Lady Myre said, 'We know all this, darling,' but I wanted to tell them more. I described my last late-night conversation with Rosie and Hank and Michael Young, when they'd said they thought they lived under Pitcairn not British law. I said how the accused men had been encouraged to plead not guilty by the defence lawyers. I agreed with the islanders that some sort of truth-and-reconciliation process would've been better for them all. They were fearful of who'd look after them if it was decided they weren't British. They couldn't make money from selling curios because where were the cruise ships now? And what use were Pitcairn stamps when there was no way of sending post.

It wasn't, I said, that I wanted in any way to defend the abusive men – far from it, it was that I didn't think this was the best route to reform. Because what was their idea of wrongdoing? I told them how Steve Christian had boasted of killing a hundred and forty fish in an hour. These men needed macho strength to survive the rigours of their crude and difficult life. What was sex for them but violence under a banyan tree? 'You can't be a girl on Pitcairn and not have sex,' Rosie'd told me. And though it was like that for the Polynesian women abducted by Fletcher Christian and Edward Young and William Brown, whose fault was it that customs hadn't changed? Who policed the place, or taught that sex should be consensual, or was concerned about what was of benefit to the islanders? The teachings of Adventism were so repressive and it was hardly possible to have candlelit dinners or to woo with flowers. 'Pitcairn men don't do wooing and flowers,' I said, 'though they like to tease ... like with a fish on a hook.'

Outside there was a thunderous crack. Kurt staggered to the deck. I swigged whisky from my flask. Through my oration Lady Myre had been sorting the counters for Dingo and Murder on the Orient Express. 'It's a pity you're such a trendy lefty, with not an iota of a sense of humour,' she said, 'because you do look so cute.' She put her hand on my thigh. 'Will you be my fish on a hook?' she said. 'I'll woo you with flowers and candlelit dinners. Though I'd quite like to have my way with you under a banyan tree.'

I wondered if death, when it came, would seem as surreal. 'We're talking about the rape of girls', I said, 'by very rough men.'

'I know, darling,' she said. 'But what can I do about it? It's an arsehole of an island. It would be better if it sank into the sea.'

I marvelled at how at ease she seemed in this dangerous situation. On Pitcairn she'd been depressed and scared of cockroaches and bed bugs. Now she seemed blithe and sublimely optimistic, as if safeguarded and in her element, whereas I was afraid.

Kurt came back and shouted, 'Yippeeee, yippeeee, the rudder's free!' He circled round and punched the air.

'You see,' said Lady Myre. 'That's what happens if you believe in Horoscopy and God.'

Apparently a counter-wave, of similar force, had dashed against the rudder and knocked it back into position. Kurt became so happy. He kept shouting yippee, and he sort of yodelled and said he was in love again. He raised a sail, fired the engine, and said now we'd blast towards Mangareva in no time. He put Jimi Hendrix on his CD player, cooked eggs and bacon, and sang along to 'Rainy Day, Dream Away'. I asked him how dangerous it had been, losing the rudder, and he said it was the most dangerous thing that had ever happened to him, ameliorated only because there was no land mass near.

The sea turned calm and so did the mood between Kurt and me. We opened a bottle of wine and set the table. Our plates and tumblers didn't slide to the floor. He even thanked me for finding those phone numbers. He said the contact had reassured him and that now he was glad we'd travelled together, though in the storm he'd thought I'd brought him bad luck.

That evening the setting sun made a path across the water. The sea was quiet enough for us to hear the squeak of the wind in the bunched bananas, now mottled by seawater, on the rigging. We talked of atolls and coral reefs and the joys of snorkelling. I supposed the *Bounty* passengers, in these same waters, had times of joy and well-being, of plain sailing in sunshine, of being dry and fed and clean. I thought how like an eighteenth-century sailor Kurt perhaps was, so close to the ocean and the sky, alert to danger, seeking always for an unknown destination.

The moon came up and the world was a clear circle. We played Lady Myre's wretched Dingo game, with many counters that belonged to Murder on the Orient Express. Her confused and mystifying rules veered from hunting with Aborigines in Tasmania, to finding Mr Ratchett's killers on a snowbound train. Kurt became tendentious over what were the real rules, but the only important one was that Lady Myre should win. I willingly lost with all grace, and her delight in victory was strange.

I had only slight apprehension about sharing a bed with her for one more night. The mood of the sea and the sky and on the boat had so changed. I felt that, though we were none of us friends, we were united by our common journey. It seemed we'd arrive at Rikitea, Mangareva's port, the following evening without more shared challenges to face. I had my letter of introduction for the Chinese shopkeeper. Soon I hoped to be alone in sunshine, absorbing the colour and life of a true Polynesian island – the scent of jasmine, stephanotis and hibiscus, garlands of flowers and shells, swimming in clear water, the tensions of Pitcairn and raging seas fading into the confusion of memory.

Lady Myre was in bed before me, the sheet under her chin. 'Hasn't it been heaven?' she said as I turned away modestly to get into my nightie.

I was unsure what she meant. 'It's certainly been memorable,' I said. I so wondered at her uninflexional mood on this journey and how it contrasted with her hysteria on Pitcairn when she'd feared she might not get her way. It was as if she had only two dimensions: contented or disturbed. She was as serene now as when half-dead with seasickness, or as when the rudder had broken in a force eleven gale and we all seemed destined for the ocean bed, or when she'd been making sexual overtures to me, a far from perfect stranger.

'I've never been so happy,' she said. 'Of all my holidays I've enjoyed this trip to Picton best.'

'Pitcairn,' I corrected her.

'Pitcairn,' she said. 'Oh yes.'

209

I clambered up to the bed. To my consternation she was naked. She'd rubbed her face with Elizabeth Arden eight-hour cream and she glistened in the moonlight.

'I so hope we can make it tonight' she said. 'It's such an opportunity, we'd be fools to miss it.' I began to say that I was frightfully sorry, but that it all made me feel frightfully awkward, and that embarrassment was a very strong emotion. 'Oh come on,' she said. 'It's hardly under-age sex.' And that made me laugh because she was fifty-five and I was old enough not to want to say how old that was.

'It has to be consensual, though,' I said. 'Not like Pitcairn.'

'Well all right,' she said. 'Let's just have a little consensual snog.'

And so I found myself surprised by the comfort of her light and tender kisses, the fresh sweet smell of her skin, and the ease and consolation of her enfolding arms. 'It's not like Pitcairn, is it,' she whispered, and I had to agree that it was not, though I couldn't overlook an underlying sense of this being worse than odd. But then the whole adventure had been rather odd.

All was calm as we approached Mangareva the following day. Mangareva means 'floating mountain'. Through her monocular Lady Myre saw birds feeding on a shoal of fish, diving and shaking their feathers, so we knew we'd soon see land.

A long silhouette of broken islands then appeared, with vegetation flowing down to the water's edge. The lagoon was turquoise and a fringe of white waves warned of the barrier reef. Bearing posts guided us for the delicate manoeuvre through the reef and into the protected bay. The ocean was now truly pacific, dappled with silver sunlight, and we could see coral in the clear water.

A dinghy with an outboard motor and two waving figures came speeding towards us. It was Kurt's yachtie friend Wilhelm, with Claudia, his Brazilian girlfriend for the year. They all hugged, and there was much excited exchange in Portuguese and German. They rolled a spliff and Kurt breathed it deep. Kurt asked Lady Myre and me if we wanted to stay on his boat in Mangareva until the air flight to Tahiti in four days. He'd only charge us fifty dollars a night.

I said I had an introduction to a friend of Rosie Christian's and that I wanted to be on land.

'And I can't stay alone with you,' Lady Myre said to him. 'I'm not a yachtie's moll, and anyway it would compromise my husband.' She gave me her smile. 'You and I must continue our journey together,' she said and it felt like a threat. But I didn't see how I could forbid her to accompany me on shore, so I looked towards the lagoon and palms and motu, the little bay of Rikitea, and the coral towers of the Cathedral of St Michael, and tried to resign myself to another island's tale.

V

OTHER ISLANDS

The benign indifference of the world

39

The Mangarevan policeman wore tight shorts and flip-flops. He stamped our passports and changed three hundred US dollars into French Pacific francs for both Lady Myre and me. She commended him on the cuteness of his bottom and I supposed that was why her wadge of received notes looked thicker than mine. Kurt told him the story of how we were all friends from Basle. I thought of Christian's fabrication to the Tahitians after he'd shoved Bligh into a boat at knifepoint. His rehearsed mendacious saga about meeting up with Captain Cook and forming a settlement on Whytootackee. And my mother's lies about her vandalised possessions. And the grand lies – about God controlling the world, and the goal of paradise, golden stories always created by someone more remote than the ordinary next-door lunatic, tall embroidered stories, because it was unconsoling to confront a bizarre molecular dance of configurations, puzzles and disintegration, where none of us, or it, was more significant than anything else.

The policeman was uninterested in why we'd arrived but said we must sleep on the boat at night. The islanders didn't want us lodging in their houses. They suspected the yachties of dealing in people, drugs and guns.

In a sad bar by the jetty Kurt introduced us to Stefan, an erstwhile Brussels accountant, with Rastafarian dreadlocks, a limp and no front teeth or money. For twelve years he'd lived on a tired-looking monohull. He caught fish, foraged for fruit and coconuts, and at night stole chickens and occasional

215

drums of fuel for his boat. The limp followed a fall from a tree he'd climbed for breadfruit. He damaged his back, had no medical insurance, was flown to Tahiti and nursed by nuns in a convent. They fed him on soup made from fishheads. It occurred to me that such soup was nutritious and that for days I'd had nothing much to eat.

Four yachts were in the bay. The fourth was captained by a dour-looking Spaniard with black curly whiskers all over his face. He had overhanging eyebrows and only his nose seemed to find its way through the foliage. Kurt said he was on the run but was vague as to what he was fleeing from, or who was in pursuit. Two women sailed with him but two women were sailing with Kurt. I thought how worse than strange the *Bounty* crew must have seemed to the Tahitians: unreadable, distinguishable only by peculiarity.

The typical yachtie women, in their twenties, scantily clad, voluptuous, dark-skinned, uncommunicative, hadn't been abducted like the first mothers of Pitcairn, but they completed a male fantasy. The men were the masters, in love with the ocean, the horizon and their boats. They were timeless voyagers, mutineers who'd turned away from society's constraints. They liked world music, drink, hashish, the wind in their sails and a distant island.

It was unsurprising the Mangarevans wanted them gone. They came from an unknown place, spoke unfamiliar languages, were unpredictable and fell out of trees.

I left the bar while Lady Myre was in the dunny, and walked to the Cathedral of St Michael that loured over Mangareva. It was a testament to the mad rule of Father Honoré Laval, a French Catholic priest who'd arrived in 1834. He'd heard of the islanders' pagan ways from whalers. He made them build this monument as proof of conversion and repentance. It was seventy-five feet high and modelled on Chartres, with seating for two thousand people – four times the current population of the island.

Laval had been received with all hospitality by King Te Maputeoa, given food and accommodation, and accorded respect. He repaid this by uprooting the island's culture. The Mangarevans were forced into Catholic marriage or celibacy and punished brutally for disobedience. Through punishment and the threat of damnation, he made them build, as well as the cathedral, a prison, a monastery and a convent. They hewed basalt, cut coral blocks from the reef, made limestone from firing coral. Fifteen hundred people died in his ten-year rule. Workers were brought in from Tahiti. All the Polynesian icons, temples, gods and holy relics were destroyed and the stone used for Laval's Catholic fantasy. King Te Maputeoa was baptised and renamed King Gregorio in homage to Pope Gregory the Sixteenth. Accounts of Laval's savagery reached the bishop of Tahiti from sailors, traders and French officials. He was summoned there in 1871, declared insane and forbidden to return to Mangareva.

Above the cathedral door was the inscription *Quis ut Deus?* – Who is as God? This strange, lofty, empty space, its vaulted blue ceiling studded with mother-of-pearl stars, its twenty high pillars, its frescoes, cornices, triglyphs, arches and friezes, was a monument to one man's arrogance and certainty. The altar and tall cross were inlaid with flower sprays of pearls and shells. Once a blue pearl of fabled size lay on the altar, and once a necklace of black pearls adorned the plaster image of the Virgin Mary.

The Mangarevans had been pearl fishers, their lives shaped by their island, the sea, bright flowers, colourful cloths, the food they found, the music they made from shells, pipes and drums. Their soul was still there in the clear lagoon, the silver sands, the small atolls with coconut palms, the huge oyster shells. Pretty children still played, their skin and eyes brown, their noses flat, their legs thick and sturdy. The girls wore garlands of shells, and hibiscus flowers behind their ears. I climbed through forests of hibiscus, candlenut, coconut and giant ferns. Chickens pecked in the aeho grass. From the convent ruins high on a hillside I followed the stone path Laval made the islanders build. It wound down to the shore. When a boat arrived they'd formed a human chain and passed provisions up the steep cliff side.

The fate of this island seemed as capricious as Pitcairn's. Good didn't triumph, but neither did bad. Nothing lasted. But the reflections of this day mattered – the smell of the sea, shifting sunlight, concealed creatures stirring among the ferns.

I called on Charlie Mo. He hovered in a store cluttered with condensed milk and rolls of linoleum. I gave him Rosie's letter and hoped he'd offer me a bed for the night away from the ocean and my companions. He read it and shook his head. It was something about a gun. He smiled and said he regretted there was no place for me to stay, but he waved his hand at green beans and sweet potatoes, offered me food from his shop, gave me a carton of kiwi juice, and asked me to take a letter to his daughter in Tahiti. She'd meet the plane.

I walked the coast with a bag of vegetables. I wondered about Chinese people on these little islands. In 1864 William Stewart, a British businessman, created a vast cotton plantation at Atimaono in southern Tahiti. He obtained a permit to import a thousand Chinese workers. Nine years later the plantation failed, he went bankrupt and the Chinese turned to market gardening, opium-dealing or general trading. Thus the accident of dispersal and the struggle to survive.

I came to another cavernous building, another memorial, like Laval's cathedral, to colonial disregard. It was a sombre, iron, windowless container, a fall-out shelter built in the 1960s by the French when they'd started blasting nuclear bombs in Polynesia. In 1962 General de Gaulle moved the French nuclear testing centre from the Sahara to his colonies in the South Pacific. No French leader would agree to these tests in his own country. The tiny atoll of Mururoa close to Mangareva was chosen as the site. Eighteen thousand French troops were stationed in Tahiti. The first bomb, a plutonium fission device, was detonated on 2 July 1966 from a barge anchored in the lagoon. The blast sucked all the water from the lagoon into the air then rained it down. It was goodbye to everything that lived in those waters – all those creatures of the deep. The islets on the encircling reef were coated with the corpses of irradiated fish and clams. The coral died.

Seventeen days later another bomb was dropped from a plane sixty miles south of the atoll. Two days after that an unexploded bomb cracked in the sea and plutonium spilled over the reef. On 2 September a 120 kiloton bomb was dropped from a helium-filled balloon. The New Zealand National Radiation Laboratory monitored heavy radioactive fallout in the Cook Islands, Tonga, Fiji and Samoa. Over the next eight years another forty-four French bombs, including five hydrogen bombs, were detonated in the skies near Mururoa. In 1974, after boycotts of French goods and airlines and proceedings against France by Australia and New Zealand in the International Court of Justice at The Hague, the next French president, Valéry Giscard d'Estaing, ordered that the tests be conducted below the surface of the sea.

Forty-six shafts were then drilled along a fifteen-mile strip to the south of the reef. The atoll was blasted to bits. Radionuclides leaked into the sea. Storms and typhoons brought giant waves that washed nuclear waste chaotically each and every way across the ocean. On Mangareva and many other islands people became ill with ciguatera – fish poisoning caused by algae that multiply when coral is killed and infect the fish's food. The sufferers endured headaches, vomiting and fever. Cancers formed: leukaemia and tumours.

I stood in the ugly, rusty, disused fallout shelter, a monument to a more heinous imposition than Laval's. All the Mangarevan people had been herded into this windowless can for forty-eight hours at a time, breathing filtered air, while the nuclear bombs were exploded. The blasts were heard on Pitcairn Island 300 miles away, they echoed under the sea, they made great tidal waves.

After this devastation came the reparation of money. An air of unearned prosperity then defined the island. Goods of every sort were sent from the 'mother country'. The islanders were given cash and prefabricated houses. Local wood and stone were no longer used in building. Every household had a four-wheeled-drive vehicle, though the island road went nowhere in particular. A new jetty was built and an airstrip with twice-weekly flights to and from Tahiti.

The Mangarevans had called their land their *fenua haohi*. It was sacred. It had been defiled. They became dependent on subsidy and compensation, their autonomy gone, forced into a sort of nuclear prostitution. The fish in the sea were still tainted. The Pitcairners might hope for links with Mangareva, but the island had nothing for them and wanted nothing from them. The Mangarevans did not think of Pitcairn. They spoke French, not English. A supply ship from Tahiti arrived regularly with fruit, vegetables and all the produce they needed.

It was dark when I reached the jetty. The moon was full and stars sparkled. Lady Myre was in the sad bar with the yachties. She accused me with her eyes and an untypical reserve. 'Where have you been?' she asked, like a disapproving spouse. A mixture of oysters, hashish and sunshine had left her pink-coloured and fractious. She'd looked for me, then gone to an atoll with the Belgian vagrant. He'd given her a large bright parrot fish to cook for our supper.

It had been a difficult day, she said. First I'd disappeared, then the nice policeman had told her she'd only be allowed two pieces of luggage on the aircraft. Kurt would have to take the rest to Tahiti or Samoa. She'd meet up with him again some sunny day. Meanwhile, if she was short of anything, she knew I'd sort it, I was such an organised little mouse.

The *Braveheart* was to arrive the following day from Pitcairn with the officials who'd served their three-month stint. Their crossing had been calm and they'd swum from the boat in the deep still ocean. They knew of our peril at sea. Captain Jolly had made radio contact with Kurt and checked with the Mangarevan policeman that we'd arrived safely.

I was pleased to be reunited with Lady Myre, alarming though her interest in me was. She made my spirits lift. Kurt took us by dinghy to his catamaran and we cooked my vegetables from Mr Mo and her parrot fish, which I hoped wouldn't give us ciguatera poisoning or worse.

The *Braveheart* arrived in the night. It sounded its siren as it crossed the reef, a forlorn echo. Another vessel with a name of affirmation: *Bounty, Providence, Resolution*. 'Our friends are here,' whispered Lady Myre. Again we shared the same tiny cabin which now was motionless on the calmest of nights. She didn't share my awkwardness about our continued intimacy. She treated me with confident familiarity, as if there were no uncertainties to allay. She didn't mind about my hesitancy as long as I accommodated her abandon.

I remarked on her golden skin now the pinkness had quietened down.

'D'you find me beautiful?' she asked, 'as I do you.' I kept

telling her to shush because sound so carried in this unfamiliar quiet.

'Oh come on,' she said, 'if the *Braveheart* can bellow like a harpy, I can scream a bit too.'

'You're not a ship,' I said with my customary perspicacity.

'O yes I am,' she replied. 'Your ship has come home.'

I thought of clichés of certainty: *I knew as soon as I saw you. It was love at first sight.* 'We'll be on the same plane to Tahiti as the *Braveheart* lot,' I whispered to her. It would leave the following afternoon but only if the weather was fine. I told her of my plan to visit the museum of anthropology in Tahiti, then fly to Tubuai in quest of evidence of Fletcher Christian's attempt to found a colony there. She said that was fine by her, and that she knew Dubai and Abu Dhabi. She always stayed in the Burj al Arab, but liked the gardens of the Hatta Fort. She kept most of the gold she'd acquired there in a safe at Little Nevish.

'Tubuai,' I said. 'Tubuai. Tubuai. Not Dubai. One of the Austral Islands in French Polynesia.' I told her it supplied vegetables to Papeete, the capital of Tahiti, and it was where Fletcher Christian had tried to build a settlement he called Fort George, in bizarre honour of the English king, after he'd dumped Bligh on the high seas.

'Try to sleep, sweetheart,' Lady Myre said. 'You'll feel like death in the morning.'

For much of the night I lay awake. She cradled against me, breathing peacefully. I supposed I was in a fix. It wasn't that she was wrong, but she so wasn't right. My journey didn't feel safe. I didn't understand myself, though I felt I understood her. I thought of Soni's arranged marriage and how the customs and expectations of a time-honoured society could sustain two disparate people. The convention of marriage. And I thought of the accepted sexual exchanges of eighteenth-century Tahitians. But two women on a random journey, who'd elided in the night... I pondered the yearning for love, the yearning to feel less alone.

In the morning she garlanded herself, Polynesian style, with shells given her by the Belgian yachtie. She'd heard that a flower worn behind one ear indicated the wearer was romantically available, and behind the other it meant she was married. She couldn't remember which ear meant what, so gardenias and hibiscus jutted from both. She and Kurt chose to go in the dinghy to the *Braveheart* in the hope of a large breakfast: eggs, bacon, sausage, chips and beans.

Alone on the boat I showered, drank coffee and sorted my clothes. I wondered about the envelope from Charlie Mo. I opened and resealed it. It was a wadge of dollars. I stared across the lagoon. Suckerfish squirmed around the hull of the boat. They ate the waste and excrement ejected into the bay. In my mind I went back to the storm, to the black, mountainous waves and frantic spray. I imagined the boat tipping over and being trapped in the hull with Kurt and Lady Myre. I thought of the *Pandora* as it crashed against the Barrier Reef, the prisoners with manacled hands and feet, powerless to swim, how Peter Heywood had said he was haunted by the cries of them floundering, desperate to be saved, and how, when the boat returned after leaving the rescued on an islet, there was silence.

In a passing moment I missed Verity. Each morning she'd tied her dressing gown at the same side, half-filled the kettle, taken the butter from the fridge to soften, let the tea brew for precisely one minute. I would not observe those things again.

Les, the Pitcairn locum checked the Belgian Rastafarian who'd fallen out of a tree. He said his spine seemed all right, he told him movements to avoid and symptoms to watch for and thought him fit to sail to his next destination, wherever that was. He also checked Claudia, Wilhelm's girlfriend, who complained of stomach pains and lethargy. He said she had chronic constipation and should eat beans and fruit and take exercise. I thought of Dr Huggan who sailed with Bligh as the *Bounty*'s surgeon, how he was always drunk and invented diseases with fantabulous names, and what a good comic character he'd be in a play but how terrifying his ineptitude for those with broken limbs or infections.

Kurt said the officials on the *Braveheart* had wanted me to leave Pitcairn because they feared for my safety. Someone might shoot me. I was a writer. I'd inveigled my way on to the island. I tried to defend myself. I said I'd mentioned early on in an email to Rosie that I was a writer. She hadn't seemed bothered. As I spoke, I thought how unpleasant self-justification sounds. Those who choose to think badly of us will do so. It's hard to change anyone's mind. The paranoia of the islanders was infectious. The officials had caught it. No one had thought to shoot me, of that I was sure.

Hank had prayed for us in the storm. His next sermon might dwell on how prayer saved our lives. It was a curious notion – a god who made the waves, then turned them to the murderous disadvantage of those with whom he was displeased. God the serial killer, the despot, the mass murderer. Yet I felt the generosity of Hank's hopes: Dear God, let those lesbians in peril on the sea be safe.

I expected Lady Myre to spend hours rationalising her luggage, as she was leaving most of it in Kurt's boat. But she randomly picked two pieces and seemed reconciled to parting from her possessions. One of the two, an embroidered holdall, was filled with artefacts she'd collected from Pitcairn's shore and claimed had belonged to the *Bounty*: a rusty washer, sixteen old nails, a gnarled piece of wood charred at one end, a broken waffle iron and various pebbles that she said were cannonballs and adzes. She also had three sprouting coconuts, a quantity of candlenuts and a large piece of obsidian. In the other case was an assortment of shoes and hats. It seemed she now had nothing to wear. 'I acquire,' she said 'and I discard. Every loss is an opportunity. I'll dress like Gauguin's girls.' I supposed she meant bare breasts and scanty skirts and I wondered about the days ahead.

Kurt ferried us to the airstrip on the far side of the lagoon. He and Lady Myre hugged, kissed and vowed to remeet in Tahiti, Samoa – wherever. She'd reclaim her luggage, she'd sail with him again. Her life, she said, was in his cabin. I wondered what he'd do with twelve cases of her clothes and things. He shook hands with me and wished me *bon voyage.*

The officials had turned into South Sea tourists, in shirts adorned with palm trees, their hair bleached by the sun, their luggage neat. Their journey had been calm and mine violent. I felt an irrational qualm of culpability: the storm happened because I shouldn't have gone to Pitcairn.

The plane was late from Tahiti and the heat intense on the dusty runway.

'Have you packed these bags yourself?' the French official asked Lady Myre as we checked at the airport desk.

'Of course not,' she replied. 'I wouldn't dream of packing my own bags. I'm Lady Myre.'

The contents of both bags were tipped out, the stones, detritus and coconuts confiscated. She was led away, over her shoulder she gave her subversive smile. She returned after about half an hour, the official had his arm round her and they were laughing.

She seemed exhilarated to be continuing her journey with only a bag of shoes. 'What a wonderful opportunity to start all over again,' she said, and I thought of the bountiful earth, feeding its creatures so that they might be fed on, again and all over again.

I looked down at islands circled by lagoons and reefs, dwarfed by the sea and distance. I could imagine how gaps occurred in the great plates grinding below the ocean bed, how magma spewed up to form these mounds of land that cooled and sank and created reefs. I thought of the *Bounty* with its methodical rigging, and how, if a prescient crewman had told Bligh about thermodynamics and digital radio and said wait two hundred years and you'll fly to Tahiti in sixteen hours in a bird-like winged machine, and you'll tell the Admiralty, voice to voice via an orbiting satellite, about Christian's transgression, he'd've thought it more fanciful than the Second Coming of Christ. I wondered what transformations there'd be two hundred years on from now: extra-corporeal travel perhaps and interplanetary harm.

Lady Myre's hand searched for mine. 'Are you scared?' she asked.

'No,' I answered. 'Why should I be scared?'

'It seems strange to be hurtling through the air,' she said, 'after all that ocean. But if it crashes we'll go together and what a comfort that will be.'

40

In the cool of Tahiti's airport lounge, observed by the *Braveheart* visitors, I slipped the envelope of dollars to the Chinese shopkeeper's daughter. The crowd was dense, but we easily met, alert to each other's expectation. She was urban and elegant. In a large Renault she took Lady Myre and me to the Sofitel hotel and tried to book us in at the discounted residents' rate.

The receptionist wouldn't agree to it, but when Lady Myre declared her title she put a garland of frangipani round her neck and accorded us a king-size bed in a luxury room with a view of the ocean. The counter was strewn with gardenias and hibiscus flowers, front-of-house allegiance to past time. Lady

Myre bagged handfuls of them. All things free she squirrelled away: paper screws of sugar, hotel stationery, shells from the seashore, twigs.

Her rank, and the self-assurance that went with it, would have served her in eighteenth-century Tahiti. Bligh consorted with the high chiefs, the *arii* – the nobles. He didn't hobnob with the lowborn *manahune*. The high chief of a tribe was revered and deferred to. Land, title and hereditary prestige belonged to him. He was carried on his servants' shoulders, food was fed into his mouth, he wore a girdle of red or yellow feathers, he could command human sacrifice.

There were many tribes, their land demarcated by the V-shaped valleys and the mountain ridges. The house of the highest chief was not luxurious, he made no display of personal possession, his servants ate the same food. Birth counted for everything, wealth for very little. The enduring symbol of a high-born family was the *marae*, the open-air stone-and-coral temple that spoke of permanence and transcended the transience of life. The gods were secondary, to do with sunlight, wind, birdsong, the sea. All the *maraes* on Mangareva had been destroyed by Laval.

The Sofitel was to a standard. The room had a huge bed with plumped pillows, a minibar, brochures about Tahitian pearls and tours, a TV in a cabinet, a view from the window of palm trees and false sand, a print on the wall of a fishing boat, an annexed windowless bathroom with little pots of shampoo and moisturiser and a hairdryer locked to the wall.

Lady Myre lay on the bed, her arms splayed wide.

'Civilisation,' she said. 'A bed, a proper lavatory, a *television*.'

I said I favoured life without television and considered it a barrier to meaningful experience.

'Then come and have a meaningful experience with me,' she said. 'You can keep your head down while I watch the chat shows.'

I ignored her and made a display of sorting my papers.

'Oh come on,' she said. 'Stop being a spoddy twerp. Let's have a candlelit bath, order normal food and wine, hire a video and indulge ourselves after our ordeal.' She fancied *Spartacus*. Didn't I just love Kirk Douglas and Jean Simmons? I probably knew Laurence Olivier was a bit of a woofer but so were most of those Romans if the truth be known. She topped up her Sprite bottle with rum from the minibar and considered the room-service menu.

I told her my plans. I wanted to see Matavai Bay where the *Bounty* had anchored, make a tour of inland Tahiti to imagine the tribal settlements where Bligh had collected breadfruit saplings, then go to an exhibition about the Polynesian canoe at the Tahiti Museum. After that I'd fly to the island of Tubuai to see Fletcher Christian's Fort George settlement, then get a plane to London.

'Whither thou goest I will go,' she said, but there was rebuke in her demeanour. She wanted sex and I wasn't complying. I wondered what she was like when she didn't get what she wanted.

'You're an awkward little Mousey,' she said. Stubborn.' Then she said I wasn't safe on my own and that she'd read of a Tahitian custom called *mafera*, where young men climbed through open hotel windows and had sex with women while they slept. I should watch out for anything untoward in the night, and unless I was certain it was her, I should call reception. She took a gardenia from behind her ear, tore it in two, gave me half and said I should do the same for her: it was a Tahitian sign of reciprocal fidelity. I pointed out I didn't have a gardenia. She told me there were all sorts of signs to make, if I was up for intercourse. The Belgian yachtie had told her about them. I should hold up the right finger of my right hand then hold my right wrist with my left hand. That would do it. Or if I bent all my fingers and wiggled them and laughed heartily...

I suggested she phone Sir Roland and tell him the good news of her safe arrival.

'I've quite forgotten poor Roley,' she said, 'now I've got you.' She suggested we order champagne and seafood risotto and mango à la Sofitel.

I told her to choose what she wanted for herself. I'd eat downstairs and see her later.

'Are you playing hard to get?' she asked as I left the room, and there was warning in those clear blue eyes.

In the foyer I used the webmail facility. Three messages from Verity were friendly and informative. She wanted to hear from me. Where was I? Was I all right? What were my plans? She'd found a flat in Colchester. She'd felt melancholy as she packed but was now busy settling in. Wasn't it strange, she said, how one spent so long in a place then moved and scarcely thought of it again? Mother's house too had been sold and her possessions auctioned, though she didn't know this. All available money was needed to provide for her care. She might live for a decade in this twilit state. She was over-sedated, kept falling, and spent her time scrabbling in a drawer looking for things she couldn't find. I sent messages of my whereabouts and safety and said I'd had a stormy journey from Pitcairn to Mangareva.

They seemed so tentative, these frail links to a receding world. It was true what Verity said: we move on, we forget. For eighteenth-century travellers the past could vanish. The *Bounty* crew fathered children on Tahiti. Peter Heywood had a fine house there with an avenue of trees. He had a partner and a child and was working on an English-Tahitian dictionary. Then Captain Edwards came in the *Pandora* and took him away in chains to shipwreck and judgement.

The dining room looked out over a swimming pool, the sham beach and coconut palms. No cutter would come to this harbour to herald wonder. I ordered cheese, fruit and wine. A stray dog scrounged the tables with a depressed look in his eyes. I gave him a crust of bread, then he wouldn't go away. He'd've stayed with me for ever. He sat and stared, ate bits of mango and custard apple but preferred the cheese. Here was the hunger of the world. No culinary fads, just a need for calories – any old fuel to stave off death for a while.

At an adjacent table an oriental-looking woman cleaned her knife and fork on a napkin, again and again. A jacket was draped on the back of the chair opposite her, so I assumed she had a companion. In American English she ordered one meal, two plates and a jug of hot water. She cut a plate of steak, then put it on the opposite place mat. She cut up salad, seemingly for herself, asked for ketchup for the chips, ate only a bread roll and drank the hot water, which she poured into a glass. The dog didn't bother with her. He knew she'd give him nothing. Again and again she bent to the floor, threw a ten-cent coin, and peered to see which way up it landed. To break her encapsulation, I asked if she was American. Her family was from China but had moved to San Francisco – she had a brother and a sister there. She said she liked Tahiti and preferred the Sofitel to the Meridian.

A waitress swore in French at the dog. It slunk to a door and watched from there.

In the foyer I booked a ticket for a tour the following day, to Lake Vaihiria and inland Tahiti, in a four-wheel-drive. Then, guilty at abandoning Lady Myre, I booked her a ticket too.

She'd left a note on the king-size bed. As I was in solitary mood, it said, she'd gone to buy clothes and explore Tahiti by night. I bathed in lavender-perfumed water, shampooed my hair and turned on CNN news. I watched President Bush say he'd never relent in defending America, whatever it took. He said he had a calling from beyond the stars to stand for freedom. I began to wish I'd stayed with Lady Myre, eaten risotto, watched *Spartacus* and enjoyed the comfort of her arms.

It felt strange, the move from the fervent ocean to this nowhere room. At around midnight I worried she might have come to harm. Her French was so peculiar. Then I thought of how spirited she was and how indestructible she seemed.

The moon was eclipsed by neon. Nor could I hear the ocean above the music from the lounge. I imagined the Tahitian canoes with a hundred and fifty paddlers, the bright stars they navigated by, the tribal chiefs decorated with red and black feathers, the clanging of coconut shells to herald attack, the sound of wooden trumpets and drums from hollowed tree trunks, the dazzle of pearl-shell knives, and bright dancing skirts...

'*Mafera,*' Lady Myre hissed as she crawled into the bed. She gave her convulsive laugh, her hands were cold and for a moment I was totally alarmed. 'I've had such adventures,' she whispered.

I was pleased she was back safely, but I didn't want to talk and be awake all night. She'd been to downtown Tahiti in *le truc* – the rough transport bus – and got herself tattooed. She wanted to show me, but I insisted she wait until morning. She said it was discreet – a bird of paradise at the base of her spine. It was very sore so I mustn't be rough with her.

I said there was no danger of that. 'Now go to sleep,' I said. And I told her how in the morning we were going inland to the crater at the centre of Tahiti, which showed how the island was formed in a huge eruption aeons ago. I said we'd travel through the valleys in the mountains where Tahitian chiefs had ruled their tribes and Bligh gathered breadfruit plants.

'What a determined explorer you are,' she said. 'But I don't care about any of that. What I like is that no one knows where we are.'

I agreed that I liked that too.

Then she began her familiar caressing, which I'd also grown to like. I asked no questions about her past, her lovers and chance encounters. Our kisses seemed part of the journey, the sea and the surprise of each day. 'What's that?' she said and guided my finger to a little lump in my armpit about the size of a clitoris.

'I don't know,' I said. 'A cyst, I suppose.' 'Probably,' she said. 'But you'd better get it checked out.'

'Yes,' I said. 'But not on Tahiti.'

'No not on Tahiti,' she said and we giggled, I don't know why, then snuggled down.

41

Those sailors in their journals didn't write the truth about their sexual behaviour and desires. They denied they were rapacious and didn't admit to homosexuality, because it was considered a crime. One nautical punishment for it was to tie the offending men together, then throw them into the sea. It made me ponder Christian's cry: that if Bligh humiliated him more he'd take him in his arms and jump overboard with him. And Peter Heywood told Sir John Barrow, who wrote about the *Bounty* in 1831, that Christian had a mitigating secret to do with his falling out with Bligh and that he himself had personal information too private to divulge.

Bligh, on his second breadfruit journey to Tahiti, logged his interest in an effeminate islander kept 'solely for the caresses of men':

The Young Man took his *hahow* or mantle off... he had the appearance of a Woman, his Yard & Testicles being so drawn in under him having the Art from custom of keeping them in this position; those who are connected with him have their beastly pleasures gratified between his thighs... On examining his privacies I found them both very small and the Testicles remarkably so, being not larger than a boys of 5 or 6 Years old and very soft as if in a State of decay or a total incapacity of being larger, so that in either case he appeared to me as effectually a Eunuch as if his stones were away.

Bligh didn't record why the young man was brought to him, or whether he gratified his own beastly pleasure between his thighs. Perhaps his curiosity about his privacies and the texture of his testicles was academic, a diversion from potting breadfruit and commanding the *Providence* crew.

The Tahitians, unembarrassed by sexual diversity, wanted to accommodate all the desires of these mariners. They hoped to benefit from their visit and they deferred to their whiter skins, but they were bewildered by their behaviour and afraid of them too. A chief became morose after his pregnant wife had sex with George Hamilton, surgeon on the *Pandora*. He feared his child would be born piebald.

Nothing prepared the Tahitians for the contagious diseases European visitors brought them: gonorrhea, syphilis, influenza, dysentery. The effect was beyond the wrath of any of their imagined gods. Imported disease halved the population in four decades. Nor had they any choice but to capitulate to the power of firearms. If they resisted the men on these warships they were destroyed, like game, by their guns. Their response was to want guns for themselves, to want the power inherent in the possession of arms.

The English mariners thought of the Tahitians as natives of an inferior civilisation. Samuel Wallis stuck a flag in the sand and named the island King George the Third Island, though it already had a name. Bligh came as an envoy of commercial enterprise: to uproot a thousand breadfruit plants in exchange for nails and beads.

42

I found it hard to decipher Lady Myre's tattoo. It looked as if someone had kicked her bottom. She was unconcerned and confident that it would 'settle down'. She'd had it done in a booth by the market that was open night and day. She said Roley wouldn't mind if she got engraved with seven continents and changed her name to Lydia. I told her tattoos were spells printed on the skin and that Taaroa was the god of tattoos. First he painted the fishes in colours and patterns, then taught the art to mortals. I said tattooing was a ceremony, which should be accompanied by music from drums, flutes and conch shells. She said her man had an electric needle, which sounded like a dentist's drill. I explained that 'Tatua' was a Tahitian onomatopoeic word for the sound of the teeth of a boned comb as it punctured the skin with pigment. For the Polynesians, I told her, tattoos were emblems of virility and status, for the sailors they were signs of macho brother-hood, or sexual involvement, but for the mutineers they became the ruddled marks for slaughter.

She said it was irritating, the way I pontificated, as if I knew everything, and that I was an encyclopaedia of useless information. If I wasn't so cute, she'd run a mile. In the tattoo booth she'd done some research on *kava*, the traditional Polynesian intoxicant. You made it by chewing the root of the pepper shrub, spitting this into a bowl, then adding coconut juice mixed with pepper leaves. The effect was befuddlement, stupefaction and sleep; it suppressed appetite, made the skin go scurfy and the eyes red and inflamed. She said I should try some. I should drink a lot of it. It might improve my libido and stop me turning into a bore. Then she ordered Buck's Fizz and shish kebab to be sent to the room.

In a huff, I phoned and booked air tickets to Tubuai, to leave in two days.

Lady Myre sat apart from me in the foyer of the Sofitel as we waited for the jeep that would take us inland. An Israeli couple who spoke only Ivrit were waiting too, and the Chinese woman from the dining room, who seemed calmer than on the previous evening. There was a display of Tahitian dancing for our entertainment. A printed blurb advertised it as a traditional welcome, the movements representing earth, wind and the rising sun. The hair of the girls was plaited with flowers, their shoulders and arms were bare, but not their breasts, their skirts were feathered, their petticoats white, their make-up by Lancôme – or was it Elizabeth Arden? To my embarrassment, after a minute Lady Myre joined in too, with a gardenia clenched between her teeth. She beckoned me to join her, but I pretended not to notice. The staff behind the counter started clapping, and guests gathered to watch the leg kick of this not-so-young Englishwoman. I was the only discomfited one. I feared identification with her, though in my heart I admired her *joie de vivre*. The Chinese woman resumed her coin-tossing when she felt secure from scrutiny.

Our French guide was impatient and his driving fast and erratic. He considered himself underpaid. Lady Myre sat in the front with him, the rest of us held on tight in the back. We followed the coast road to Matavai Bay, where the *Bounty* had anchored. There was only a glimpse of a grey, metallic, ferrous-oxide beach shrouded with rain, the coastline sprawl of a modern town, and no ship on the horizon. The driver wouldn't let us get out of the jeep. There wasn't time, he said. He turned inland along a rough track. On either side were steep mountains with white clouds trapped on their jagged peaks. He looked over his shoulder to inform us: 'We will go to the central crater of the island. To the Papeeno River. To the hydroelectric power station. And then we will return to the hotel.'

'Slow, please, slow,' said the Chinese lady. He took no notice or didn't hear. 'Papeete means "City of Springing Water",' he turned to say. 'There are five hundred waterfalls on the island.' The Israeli couple addressed him excitably in Hebrew. 'Hoopla,' Lady Myre sang as we hit a pothole. She'd shown the same enthusiasm in a small boat at sea in a force twelve gale. The Chinese lady began talking to herself in her original tongue.

I looked at the green valley and retreated to thoughts of Bligh and the gardener David Nelson in breeches, waistcoats and neckcloths, setting up camp by the streams and potting breadfruit plants; of the tribal chiefs, tattooed, long-haired, wrapped in cloth and decorated with feathers; of the women cooking on ovens of stones. It seemed strange there were now no settlements in these valleys, so fertile with waterfalls and dense vegetation.

The tribal Tahitians had felt such connection to this land. To give birth a woman squatted on her heels with a helper behind her pushing the child out. The umbilical cord was then buried in the land to become the land. Taaroa was their god of first creation. For aeons of time he'd lain in the darkness of his shell, then cracked it open as he pushed it apart. The upper half became the dome of the sky, the lower became the foundation of the earth, the seabed, the earth's crust. Not so far off, I thought, from Gaia, the biosphere, the thin spherical shell around the incandescent centre of the earth. Other Tahitian gods created stars, the sea, islands, the winds and tides. They filled the sea with fish, the sky with birds. Then followed more interventionist gods: of thieving, canoe-building, tattooing.

Festivals of thanksgiving and prayers were to celebrate the ripening of fruit, the harvest, the averting of disaster. A booby bird alighting on a turbulent sea meant the water would calm, the sight of an albatross meant luck for canoeists, the white sea swallow was a messenger of peace. In tribes they worked with the island. It lived with them. They interpreted the moonlit stillness, the fall of meteors, the flight of clouds. Unseen gods inhabited the hills, woods and seashore. They heard the cry of spirits in the screech of nightbirds, felt them in gusts of wind, tasted them in the flesh of crabmeat.

Tahitian men were as murderous as their visitors. They fought with spears, clubs, stones, bows and arrows, and axes honed from pearl shell. They ran their victim through with a rasp made from the serrated backbone of a stingray or with a forked stick studded with sharks' teeth. A victor might beat his victim's body to a pulp, cut a slit through it large enough for his own head, then wear it poncho-fashion. If a chief fathered a child with a woman who was not of his class, it was killed before it drew its first breath. The physically infirm were rejected. The insane were avoided but respected as inspired or possessed by some god.

The death of those who were loved was met with great display. The bereaved gashed themselves and chopped off their own finger joints. The corpse was bathed and rubbed with scented oils, and prayers were said to protect the departing soul. When the soul had left, the body rotted away. Its skull was then polished and stored.

We stopped for a minute at the crater, a huge hole lined with ash. I thought of the sound of that explosion and the colour of fire, and how the night after Christian's coconut saga the volcano at Tofua erupted as the *Bounty* passed in the dark, so he couldn't jump ship because the crew came up on deck to watch.

Lady Myre ignored me and photographed the driver. He gave up telling us about Tahiti. He picked a large taro leaf in which rainwater had collected and told us to do the same. He then took birdseed from the jeep and strewed it around. Chickens scurried out from the bushes and a parakeet flew down. He said rats had destroyed many birds of the valley.

The rain washed into me. I hated the bumpy drive and I

wasn't at ease with this group. I felt I'd lost the path to Pitcairn and the fragments of connection to the past. And I grieved the gap that was growing between Lady Myre and me. I looked at her straight back and ridiculous rainhat and felt sad.

43

Lady Myre didn't return to the hotel after the tour. The French guide showed her the town. In the afternoon I went alone to the exhibition about the Polynesian canoe. The Museum of Tahiti was in a coconut grove by the lagoon with a view through trees to the island of Moorea.

I walked past displays about the birth of the island. Projected on to a screen was the eruption of the volcano and the sinking of the reef. Behind glass were large pieces of dead coral, sponges, the shells of sea urchins and lobsters, models of fish from the lagoon, photographs of white sharks, tiger sharks, tuna, flying fish and dolphins. The 'War Room' was filled with slings, spears, truncheons and clubs, wooden gods and feathered headdresses, drums and nasal flutes and conch shells. There were contrived displays of games, celebrations and funerals, showcases of tapa cloth made from beaten bark, sandals made from rope, crowns adorned with pearls and dolphins' teeth, fans of coconut-palm fronds, tiaras of seashells and tortoise shells, bracelets of woven hair, rings made from tropical birds' feathers. There was a whole room about tattooing; all the instruments – the combs of tortoiseshell and bone, the little mallets to punch the comb into the skin – the geometric designs for warriors and chiefs, patterns for rites of passage and their meanings.

Something of what Tahiti had been was here behind glass. I thought of my walk through Harrods when I was looking for Rosie's blouse. The same sense of so much stuff and all of it temporal. None of it kept death away.

In the *Va'a* exhibition was a reconstruction of a wondrous-looking ocean-going canoe forty feet long, with huge steering paddles and bailers and stone anchors. There were outrigger paddling canoes of the sort used for fishing expeditions and outrigger sailing canoes for voyaging across the sea. The painstaking work of construction was shown: how the planking was sewn to the hull with ties of coir and the wood inlaid with mother-of-pearl, how pandana leaves were plaited to serve as sails, and fishbones used as needles. Samuel Wallis, when he reached Tahiti in 1767, ordered the destruction of all the canoes moored in Matavai Bay.

The Tahitians had used the ocean as a thoroughfare. They sailed with the protection of gods, saw divine providence in the rising sun, were beckoned home by a tranquil sea. Again it seemed to me that those who went to Pitcairn would not have been deterred by the burning of the *Bounty*. Pitcairn was not their home. They'd return to where their umbilical cord was buried.

Wanting tea and cake and souvenirs, I got *le truc* to the market. I bought black pearls and bright pareus and took photos of stalls of pineapples, mangoes, breadfruit, fish and flowers. I wished that Lady Myre was with me. Without her, all that I saw belonged to museums. She was my muse. Her smile lit up my life. I hurried back to the hotel. She was not in our room. I found her stretched out on a lounger by the pool with a Tahitian cocktail and a copy of *Hello!* magazine. I asked her if she'd have supper with me. She gave me a cold look, but to my relief she said she would.

44

Lady Myre asked if I thought the wings of the plane wide enough to get us all the way to Dubai. And she was surprised to be served no more than a beaker of banana juice, which she fortified with rum. She wore clothes acquired in the Tahiti market: a trouser suit printed with unlikely animals living under coconut palms and a panama hat adorned with shells. Once again I told her that Tubuai was a small island in the Austral Group where Fletcher Christian and his wayward crew had made unsuccessful attempts to settle. She told me to hold her hand and try to keep my thoughts about Fletcher Christian to myself.

She must have known we weren't heading for Dubai in this small twin-engined plane. I suspected she wasn't confused at all. I never knew when she was teasing or telling the truth. It wasn't that I thought she lied, it was just that the truth was an uncertain concept. I put it down to her time as entertainment staff with the Shaw Savill Line, and all those years in provincial rep – shooting herself every night for three months in *Hedda Gabler*.

We landed to a view of a perfect South Sea island, so other than Pitcairn: white sand ringed with palms, a clear, still lagoon and surf breaking over the encircling reef. Melinde greeted us with garlands of flowers, took us to her house, showed us our bedroom and place to wash and where to hire bicycles. From the window was a view of the bay and swaying palms.

Lady Myre wanted to rest and listen to her iPod, so I walked to the shore. At my feet were big, curled oyster shells. A chicken rooted for ants in the sand. There was a crude carved notice nailed to a post: *Baie Sanglante La Bounty 30 Mai 1789*. It wasn't hard to imagine the anchored ship, the Tubuaians grouped to watch, the pirogues paddling out, the persuasion of nails and feathers, the astonishment and fear of the chief who went on board and for the first time ever saw pigs, goats, dogs and even a cow. It was unsurprising that a young man stole the azimuth compass when he heard of its magical use. And then the panic: the Tubuaians throwing stones, Christian ordering fire, a dozen islanders killed, the clear water of the bay stained red. Baie Sanglante – the Bay of Blood.

Now fishes weaved around in bright, translucent water. I walked along the shore to the site of Fort George. There was little to see of Christian's settlement – only a field one hundred feet square, a wire enclosure, a few ditches, a notice board. The site was idyllic, near the river, by the sea. The climate was gentle, the soil fertile. Here was all that was needed for survival, except trust, safety and fairness. It was hard to imagine how Christian thought a fort with a drawbridge and moat feasible in such a place, in the name of an English king. It seemed as anomalous and bizarre as Laval's cathedral on Mangareva. But the Tubuaians weren't going to help build Christian's folly. They were united in hostility, they'd destroy

245

it when they could. This field was a testimony to a desperate venture by men on the run, cornered by wrongdoing and with no place to go.

I walked for a while along a mountain path, on a carpet of pine needles, past pale-green firs, breadfruit trees and unfurling ferns. I saw butterflies, iguanas and feral cats. Time and the sea eroded all things. Change happened in so many ways: by riding roughshod over the lives of others, by the perversion of gunfire and by the volcano's answer to the might of arms.

Lady Myre seemed content that the island had all the features of a South Sea brochure: coconut palms and silver sand. She sang as she cycled on her hired bike 'I am the Wife of Mao Tse-tung' by John Adams, 'When All is Said and Done' by ABBA. When she complained of thirst, we stopped by the shore to get liquid from a fallen coconut. She stabbed inconsequentially at its husk with scissors from her manicure set. Waist-high in the green water of the lagoon was a figure from Polynesia's past. Above his head he held a five-pronged spear. He stood as motionless as a heron waiting for a fish. '*Monsieur*,' called Lady Myre. He turned, the spear still shoulder high, his body glistening in the sun, his hair tied into a ponytail, his shoulders rippling. She beckoned him and he waded towards her. His wet thin shorts clung to him. His arms, chest and calves were all symmetrically tattooed.

'*Monsieur. Pouvez-vous me dire* how on earth I get into this coconut? *Là?*' asked Lady Myre gesticulating with her scissors. 'Or *là?*' The fisherman took the green drupe from her, pounded it against a protruding spike, tore at its husk then handed it back.

'What now?' she asked and looked at him helplessly.

He pointed to the growing end of the seed: '*Les yeux et la bouche*' – he pointed to his eyes and mouth, then made a stabbing motion at these soft parts of the seed. Lady Myre pierced a hole in the *bouche* with her scissors and to her surprise could then drink from it.

I thought of Bligh and Fletcher Christian. 'Damn your blood you have stolen my coconuts,' Bligh was supposed to have said. 'I was dry. I thought it of no consequence. I took one only,' was Christian's answer.

The fisherman waded back into the green lagoon. Beyond him was the white fringe of the reef. Again he held his spear at shoulder level. He drove it into the sea then turned with a fish the size of a small canoe. It glinted silver – as silver as his spear and as the sunlight on the sea.

'Oh *bravo bravissimo*,' called Lady Myre. 'Gosh, what a dish,' she said to me. I was unsure what she meant.

He waded slowly from the sea with no display of pride beyond his innate demeanour of pride. He gestured we should follow him and we wheeled our bicycles to his house. It was built of bamboo with walls woven from coconut leaves. There was a lean-to cookhouse beside it. A canoe rested on the ground. He had built it all himself. He had his own water hole, he cooked on stones set in a bed of ashes, he wove his baskets and mats, made traps for snaring birds, grew vegetables and herbs, he crushed bark and leaves to soothe grazes.

In a mix of French and mime he told Lady Myre that his wife had died in childbirth a year ago. The fish was for his five children's supper. He wrote his name, Tahuaiare, in the sand and drew a heart. He said he had many names. She gave her name as 'Silver'. I wondered if she was mad. He said she was to call him Tahu and that he was looking for a wife. A boy, Muti, brought a mat for her and me. Tahu put two garlands of flowers round her neck. Another child brought a basket of yams, bananas and pineapple. Tahu prepared a fire beneath the stones to get them hot. His eldest daughter, Yolande, seasoned the fish. She was seven.

Lady Myre admired the many rings in Tahu's ears. He'd pierced them with a thorn from a lemon tree. He offered to do the same to hers. He told her of a cannibal woman, Hina, who lived in a cave high on Mount Taitaa, and used a net to catch her victims. He talked of the time when Tubuai was ruled by a king and there were chiefs of all the districts. All the time he talked he watched. He watched the sea, noting its colour and the apparent direction of currents. He watched for birds, for particular cloud formations, for the colour of the sky and the direction of the wind.

He had an accordion and while the stones heated, he serenaded her. She started singing, 'Bali Hai will call you, any time any day.' The children banged stones together to accompany her. I left them to it. I said I'd agreed to eat with Melinde and that I wanted to see more of the island before it got dark. As I cycled off, I marvelled how she went straight to the heart of wherever she was. Then subverted it.

I followed the coast road. Every hundred yards there was a sign: *Silence. Culte.* Then a church built by Mormons, Latter Day Adventists, Catholics, all keen to save the Polynesians from their own gods and known imagination. The buildings were well-tended but lifeless and not intrinsic to the island.

Melinde gave me fish, potatoes and bananas. I told her Lady Myre had met a friend and was having a picnic by the sea. She said she supposed that would be Tahu, and that he was a nice man who would look after her. She talked of the island: how there used to be crops of coffee, vanilla, manioc, copra; how the islanders would thatch their houses with coconut leaves and burn coconut oil perfumed with grated sandalwood in their lamps. She said now French Polynesians were like fledglings in a nest with their mouths open. If France, the mother bird, didn't feed them, they'd starve. The crops were gone, the land eroded. 'The French gave us the bomb,' she said. 'If you live in Normandy, you ask, "Why should we pay taxes to subsidise French Polynesia?" I answer, "Why didn't you let off the bomb in Normandy? You could never pay us enough."'

Lady Myre didn't come back to Melinde's that night. Lying awake in another strange bed, I missed the comfort of her arms. I thought of the way she sang and danced and smiled and how I never knew what she was going to do next. And then I thought of my mother and how I didn't know how to contact her. She was like a spectre, dead within life, and I couldn't help her. I felt my journey was over and that it was time to return, though I didn't know quite what that would mean, or what I'd come for, or what I'd achieved.

In the morning I cycled back to where I'd left Lady Myre. She was standing in the lagoon with Tahu, both of them statuesque with spears raised. I watched, wondering if they'd catch a fish, hoping they wouldn't for the fish's sake. After a while she turned and saw me and waded towards me. She said she was very all right and she'd wed Tahu like a shot if it wasn't that Roley was such a darling. He was teaching her to spear fish and she'd already caught a mahi mahi. He'd given her a little house all to herself. He was a perfect gentleman and he wooed her with gardenias and oyster shells. She said she'd found the heart of Polynesia.

I told her I was returning to Tahiti the following day and then to London.

'You must do what you want to do, Mousey,' she said.

'Are you coming with me?' I asked. That was as near as I could get to saying I hoped she would. She said she wasn't ready, that this was an adventure and she wanted to live it.

Then she told me I was a disappointment to her. She felt I'd gone cold on her and I never said anything nice about her. And it bored her rigid the way I went on about the mutiny on the *Bounty* and chaos theory. She said I used this stuff as a barrier to keep life out. It was now that mattered not the eighteenth century. At first she'd thought I was cute and up for it, but I should learn the lesson that if I couldn't give more I'd always be on my own. 'We meet on a ship,' she said. 'We make the best of whatever feeling is between us. But you – you let everything slip through your fingers.'

I took my bicycle back to the hire shop then sat by the shore and looked out to sea. The horizon sixteen miles away was the limit of our vision, so Captain Dutt had said. It shimmered and invited, though there were no ships on it. Go the sixteen miles and there'd be another sixteen miles. No end to the limitation of it. I wondered what my journey would have been if I hadn't met Lady Myre sitting on her pot noodles at Tauranga harbour. More focused, perhaps, but as adrift as I now felt.

I thought of Bligh and Christian and how they hadn't made the best of whatever feeling was between them. I imagined the mutineers scanning the horizon beyond the reef, dreading the ship of retribution yet expecting it too. In the afternoon I packed my Eagle Creek bag and caught the plane back to Tahiti.

45

And then a car to Tahiti airport, in transit, wanting to be on my way. Harold Wing had again rearranged my flights. I'd change planes in Los Angeles, then to London and then... There'd be waiting at airports, but waiting in a departures lounge wouldn't be much different from waiting somewhere else. I extravagantly tipped the taxi driver. He looked like Chief Otoo with a halo of black hair. I'd no more need of Pacific francs. He gave me a large black bead in appreciation and said it was a pearl.

The ritual of check-in and boarding gates didn't seem like travel: a disembodied voice announcing delays and closing of gates, the checking of papers, emptying of pockets, the scrutiny of baggage. I asked for an aisle seat near the front of the plane.

I waited to fly over the knocked-about world, to go through

time zones, two Wednesdays, so many Wednesdays, and then no more. Local time, estimated arrival time. The names of places on a screen: Kupang, Malang, Banjarman. The names of those long-gone much-raped pretty girls: Mauatua, Vahineatua, Teio, Faahotu...

I thought of Bligh and those starving men. At the edge of life and death. Drenched with rain and seawater, guided by the stars the sun and the moon, battered by waves, wringing out their tattered clothes, dividing a morsel of bread, a captured bird, into eighteen equal pieces. 'Who shall have this?' Gate 28 now closing.

I wondered where she was, that Lady Myre. Had she married Tahu, or met up again with Kurt, or Garth the step-brother? Had Sir Roland sent a ship to collect her? I scanned the waiting passengers and thought I saw her, that straight back and rolling walk, that modulated embarrassing voice: 'Drivah you're going too fast.' I wondered why I missed her, she was so unsuitable, it wasn't rational love. But her indifference to uncertainty had allayed my confusion, and she was so good at the thrill of the moment, the fruits of the day.

Images of a journey: her singing on the coach to Tauranga, seasick on the deck of Kurt's catamaran, wasps swirling round her, gardenias in her hair – all of it gone. Thanks for all your generous love and thanks for all the fun. The words of some song. And such a yearning on my part for something I'd never find. Did she collect things because of the elusiveness of the moment – the stones from the beach, travellers that passed by – whereas I let it all slip away? Would passengers please proceed to Gate 34, now boarding.

As she stood in the lagoon at Tubuai, a spear in her hand, in her mind's eye she was a Polynesian fisherwoman. Or dancing with Captain Dutt, how amused the sailors seemed. The chaos of her sermon on Pitcairn, her calm in the storm. The storm was so much more than any violence in my heart but it hurt me to remember the silkiness of her skin, the comfort of her arms, the sweetness of her kisses. We shared a journey, it ended, we went our separate ways. I wondered if she too in a way was seeking home.

You have to be so close to one person only, to hear the beat of a heart. A catamaran with a broken rudder, the crack of huge waves against the boat. Her cries too, and mine. Beyond the fear I'd rather have died by drowning in those seas, in her arms, on that night, than in the old people's home.

But the morning came and the danger passed and the sea was calm and the sun shone. And so again goodbye. Goodbye to the crew of the *Tundra Princess*, to Verity, to mother, to the moon and the Pole Star and the wasps in the hymnal. Goodbye to my brothers, to Jackie the tame frigate bird, to those who chose to go to sea but didn't choose to drown. And goodbye to the journey and the elusive moment, for there is no stillness in the turning world.

In a discarded English newspaper at Los Angeles airport I read a letter from a distant relative of William Bligh's, Maurice Bligh of Sittingbourne. Hollywood film-makers, he wrote, blamed his ancestor William Bligh, RN, FRS, for the mutiny on the *Bounty*. They should realise there never was a mutiny, only a 'piratical seizure'. There was no evidence that Bligh was a tyrant. 'Fletcher Christian wasn't an aristocrat like Marlon Brando seemed to think, but a sweaty, faceless, badly educated poor boy from a bankrupt family. If he looked like the only known portrait of his son Thursday October Christian he had problems.'

This later Bligh was partisan about his great-great-great-uncle, thrice removed, whom others called Bounty Bastard Bligh. I wondered about the favours Bligh gave and took from Christian and Heywood both. Heywood had connections in high places, so he didn't swing from the gibbet for helping Christian mutiny. Lord Hood, who presided at the trial, was a family friend. He took him as a midshipman on his ship the *Victory*. Heywood then had a long and successful naval career and became a captain. The men who died 'hanged by the neck', found guilty of mutiny – John Millward, Thomas Ellison, Thomas Burkett – didn't have connections to bail them out. Bags over their heads, nooses round their necks, a shot from a gun, ropes pulled, their bodies swung for two hours in the rain.

Millward had said that a musket was forced on him in the fracas of the mutiny. Thomas Ellison said, 'I was no more than between sixteen and seventeen years of age when this was done.' Thomas Burkett left a son on Tahiti.

So many people in the departures lounge, whatever the time of day or night. All on their way. The women on the *Bounty*, menstruating, unable to keep clean, unable to get away, caught in a man's world. The eight-year-old girl who saw John Adams despatch Matthew Quintal with a hatchet and the blood spatter the walls. My own mother, so old, beyond reach. She had a fine face, high cheekbones, an engaging laugh. I wished I'd asked for a photograph. The stowaway boy on Bligh's second breadfruit journey who died when he reached England. The quiet gardener, David Nelson, who worked to make the breadfruit enterprise a success. Ridiculous Dr Huggan, all the time drunk and disreputable. The sea closing over floundering men when the *Pandora* was wrecked and the boats were full.

Christian claimed he'd only taken one coconut because he was thirsty. One thing led to another. If everything connects, who can know it all. The abducted Tahitian girls climbing the Hill of Difficulty, losing even their names, weeping as they saw the *Bounty* burn, enduring sex, giving birth, tearing down their houses to build a boat to escape captivity. The Pitcairn girls who couldn't say they'd been caught like fish by the Pitcairn men. The animals... Pigs shoved over the cliffs because of some loony notion of God's will. Cows and goats tethered and sliding as the waves rolled. The cats who'd jumped ship when they spied land, to be chased and castrated centuries later by a rapist with a chisel.

And I, moving among facts, half-truths and illusions, not a scribe of certainties, with a central image of a rudderless boat, at the mercy of the sea, at the mercy of the storm, striving for direction to an undirectional journey, most at home if there was a joke. The fumes from a plane on the runway gagged my throat. Surabaya, Solo City, Singapore now boarding, gates now closing, arrival time unknown.

46

I boarded another Boeing 747. I glanced to the left as I walked to the right. I turned when I saw that blonded head. She was stretched out on her reclining seat, iPod applied, a Bellini and almonds on her personal side table, the white sapphire glinting, demurely dressed in Rosie's blouse and a black silk trouser suit, reading the *Wall Street Journal*.

'Hello, Mousey,' she said. 'Are you going to steerage class?' I said I supposed I was. She asked me to be a darling and get her bag from the overhead locker, she wanted to file a nail. I handed her a small black case. She said she'd bought essentials in LA while staying at Mulholland Drive, but couldn't wait for Martina and the row of possibles at Harrods. 'I told you Roley would sort things,' she said. 'He always does. He's such a dependable old dog.' I said I'd imagined her married to Tahu and baking fish on stones in Tubuai for his five children. 'Please, Mousey,' she said. 'Do I look like a Polynesian native? When push comes to shove I'm strictly Room 500 at the George Cinq.'

Then she told me I'd played silly buggers, going off on my own, leaving her with those yachties, then snubbing her at the Sofitel. 'I'm far too nice and straightforward for a headfuck,' she said, and now there was ice in those translucent eyes. But she said she'd no regrets. It had been her best holiday ever, apart from when she went white-water rafting in Ecuador, and if again she was marooned on a scarcely inhabited island, or stuck at sea in a small boat in a force twelve gale, she hoped she'd have me in bed with her to get her through the night.

What could I say? I thanked her for all the love and all the fun. She turned to the shares page of her paper. I made my way to my seat.

AFTERWORD

I CANNOT SAY, 'All characters in this book are entirely fictitious and bear no resemblance to real people alive or dead.' Perhaps I should say, 'Any character in this book bears only questionable resemblance to a real person, alive, unborn or dead.' I've hovered between fact, half-truth and fiction. The 'I' of author and narrator are not one and the same, but nor are they entirely distinct. I have kept to the public record for facts about eighteenth-century sea voyages and the felonies of present-day Pitcairn men, but the narrative voice is invented. The narrator's relatives, love affairs and preoccupations are not mine. Yes, I travelled to Pitcairn on a cargo ship, stayed on the island, left on a catamaran, but my actual journey was not as written here. Or some of it was like it, but different too. So in answer to the unasked question, what really happened? Well, I made a voyage, half-remembered, half-imagined and open to interpretation.

My gratitude is unequivocal. All thanks to Pedro Niada who prompted me to this journey. Pedro lives on Robinson Crusoe Island, 360 miles west of Chile. He was my guide when I stayed there in 2000 to write *Selkirk's Island*. In 2003 he sailed the South Pacific. In an email he told me of Pitcairn's remoteness, rough terrain and strangeness. His email coincided with news reports about crimes of rape and assault of Pitcairn girls. The accused men had the same surnames as the eighteenth-century mutineers from HMS *Bounty*.

Pitcairn, the mutiny on the *Bounty*, chaos theory, and a sense of being drawn to an isolated faraway island all resonated in my thoughts and feelings when Pedro sent his friendly email and like a mutineer I wanted to sail with the wind, because of a private chaos of heart.

Thanks too to Philippa Brewster. Halfway through working on this book I slipped into a cafard. Philippa called round every second Thursday for coffee and pages in progress. With her help I got back on course.

I revised my draft manuscript in the writers' residence on Chloride Street in Broken Hill in the Australian outback. It was an ideal retreat. My thanks to Marvis Solfield, Broken Hill's library manager, for arranging the residency and to Gillian Parry for recommending me.

This is the third of my books designed by Peter Campbell. This time there's the added delight of his illustrations for the text. His collaboration reflects our abiding friendship. I'm grateful to Alan Samson, publisher at Weidenfeld & Nicolson, for his help and guidance. Georgina Capel, my agent, as ever gave her much valued support and advice. Anne Clements read the manuscript and made many a discerning comment and improving point. Naomi Narod watered my plants while I travelled.

And all thanks to my friends in Devon. There is a real Mill Cottage where Pam Mills lets me write. The swallows do return each year. And at the top of the lane is the Greenshields' farm, where at the end of many a working day I've sat by the log fire in the inglenook to drink a glass of wine and to chat and joke with Renate and Annie.

London, Broken Hill, Devon, 2006